# THE PLOUGH AND THE PEN

D1606884

# THE PLOUGH AND THE PEN

## PAUL S. GROSS AND THE ESTABLISHMENT OF THE SPOKANE HUTTERIAN BRETHREN

by
**Vance Joseph Youmans**

Winner of Eastern Washington State Historical Society's 1993 Joel Ferris
Award for best historical work on the Inland Empire of the Pacific Northwest

with a Foreword by
**Prof. John A. Hostetler**

**Parkway Publishers
Boone, North Carolina
1995**

**Parkway Publishers**
**Box 3678**
**Boone, North Carolina 28607**

Cover Photo: Paul S. Gross (photo courtesy of Spokane Hutterian Brethren).

Library of Congress Cataloging-in-Publication Data


Youmans, Vance Joseph, 1963-

    The plough and the pen : Paul S. Gross and the establishment of
the Spokane Hutterite colony.

       p.     cm.

    Includes bibliographical references and index.
    ISBN 0-9635752-5-2

    1. Spokane Hutterian Brethren--History.  2. Gross, Paul S.
3. Spokane Region (Wash.)--Church history.  I. Title.

BX8129.H8Y68  1994
 289.7'3--dc20
                                     94-21473
                                      CIP

# CONTENTS

# LIST OF ILLUSTRATIONS
(following page 82)

1. Sixteenth century woodcut, depicting the styles of dress and the design of the bruderhofs of early Hutterites.
2. Pincher Creek Colony, Alberta, shortly after its founding in 1926.
3. Wolf Creek Colony, site of the first Dariusleut community in North America, showing the standard layout of a typical modern Hutterite colony.
4. Harvesting at Pincher Creek Colony with the first three self-propelled combines manufactured by Massey Harris.
5. William Gross, manager of the Spokane Hutterian Brethren.
6. A timeless scene of Hutterite life at Spokane Colony.
7. Women in the garden at Pincher Creek Colony, in the 1940s.
8. Hutterites in traditional dress seem anachronistic amid the modern farm buildings of Spokane Colony.
9. Paul S. Gross, the farmer.
10. Paul S. Gross, the trapper.
11. Paul S. Gross, the historian.
12. The farm in Lind, which the Hutterites leased in 1956.
13. Spokane Colony, shortly after it was built, circa 1961.
14. Spokane Colony, three decades later. The community, as well as the shade trees, have flourished.
15. A sampling of antique Hutterite books still in use.
16. As in many Hutterite communities, the schoolhouse at Spokane Colony doubles as a church. Here a family enters the schoolhouse for evening services.
17. The future leaders and followers of the Spokane Hutterian Brethren. How will they fare in the 21st century?
18. Always the teacher, Paul S. Gross draws the attention of his young audience to one of the many newspapers to which the colony subscribes.
19. The intellectual legacy continues: grandson Phillip Gross listens as Paul S. Gross, semi-retired, reads from *The Hutterite Way*.
20. Mothers and children of the Spokane Hutterian Brethren in a moment of relaxation.

# LIST OF FIGURES

# FOREWORD

The Hutterites originated in 1528 during the Protestant Reformation. They are one of three surviving Anabaptist groups (the other two being the Mennonites and the Amish) which share a body of common beliefs, including adult or believer's baptism, nonresistance or pacifism, and simple living. The Hutterites are unique among Anabaptist groups in their practice of communal ownership of property and communal living. Their search for religious freedom has taken them from Moravia (today the Czech Republic) to Slovakia, Hungary, Romania, Russia, the United States and Canada.

The Hutterites demonstrate a remarkably stable pattern of communal living in a socially unstable world. Social stability is achieved by a combination of factors. First of all, material, spiritual, intellectual, social, and psychological needs are met within a community that has an orderly, predictable existence. The community's expectations of its individual members are clearly defined, and most individuals are able to meet these expectations. Also, the Hutterites are successful in training and preparing their children for communal living. Training is consistent and continuous in all age groups. A certain amount of human failure is tolerated within each group, while strong reinforcement is provided by the group. And the Hutterites are effective in managing their adolescents, including them in family life, work, and social responsibilities. Most of the young people are able to meet the standards set by the community.

The Hutterite communities are neither utopian in thought or practice nor free from problems or crises. They have had all of them. They have survived because they have had more than sufficient resources to weather the disasters common to communal societies. The early period of prosperity and growth in the sixteenth century, in which large numbers of refugees joined the movement, is very different from the twentieth century experience, which is characterized by natural increase and unhindered expansion. As the wider society around them has changed, they have been able to adapt to new technology and even solve problems of their own making.

Fifty years ago, only one book on the Hutterites was available in the English language. That book was *The Hutterian Brethren* (1931) by John Horsch. Today there are scores of books on the Hutterites. Any graduate student or researcher working with published sources must read a large number of books and monographs and must use archives and libraries in several states and foreign countries.

With the publication of Joseph Eaton's books and articles, beginning in 1952, scientific interest in the Hutterites accelerated. Specialized studies of interest to researchers have included the following: comparative study of communes, medical studies of various kinds, mental health and personality, minority status and prejudice, demography, genetics, social change and social stability, agricultural economy, birth, death, education, legal and legislative reports, language, linguistics, and hymnology. All of this research activity has given Hutterites a celebrity status and a positive identity. If there is any void in Hutterite research, it is the publication of individual colony histories. This volume by Vance Joseph Youmans helps to fill that void, and is an excellent model for doing historical research on individual colonies.

The history of the Espanola Hutterite community and the movement of colonies into the state of Washington is inseparable from the life work of Paul S. Gross. Paul S. Gross is an Anabaptist-Hutterite historian who has informed many scholars in the academic community at home and abroad. But he is more than a historian: he is an ordained elder, a gifted leader and policy maker, an author, and a bookseller. He is a peacemaker among his own people, as well as a fighter against the atomic bomb and a pacifist. He is a pamphleteer, a publisher, a salesman, and a theologian. And, among the northwestern states and provinces, he is an accomplished trapper.

This book, *The Plough and the Pen*, brings together the many elements that go into making an enduring Hutterite colony.

John A. Hostetler
Professor Emeritus of Anthropology and Sociology
Temple University
Philadelphia, Pennsylvania 19122

# PREFACE

There exists in North America a particular group of people known as the Hutterian Brethren. They are a contemporary embodiment of the Radical Reformation whence they originated. Their communities, or *bruderhofs*, are unique enclaves of living history. Their dress and language, indeed their entire existence, speak of a different era. Quiet agriculturalists, the Hutterites remain apart from the mainstream of modern society. Most people have neither seen nor read of them. Yet they are present in our midst, unobtrusive and peaceful, continuing their rich heritage with determination.

A group of these colorful people established a community on the outskirts of Spokane, Washington in 1960, having already farmed in the Big Bend area of Washington for four years. They came from Canada seeking suitable farmland on which to continue their agrarian tradition.

Having had previous exposure to the Hutterites in Montana, I made initial contacts with the manager, or "boss," of the Spokane Colony to enquire about the possibility of writing a short history of their community. It soon became evident that individual colony histories are rare, a missing link in Hutterian historiography. Since it is impossible to comprehend twentieth century Hutterianism without a working knowledge of its history, I realized that I was embarking on a formidable project. What began as a succinct story of a thirty-two year period developed into a historical investigation of considerable proportions. I was told that "something is written about the Hutterites every day." Sources ranging from sixteenth century chronicles to contemporary newspaper articles bespeak of an intricate history wherein events a continent away often affect the spiritual and temporal lives of the Hutterian Brethren.

My research began with a literature review of local sources. Aside from newspaper articles in the *Spokesman-Review*, the regional libraries afforded only limited information of a very general nature. The dearth of printed material in the area was countered by a wealth of oral history available at the colony itself. This led to a series of interviews, which eventually became the primary resource for this book. I interviewed other local sources, including lawyers, building contractors, neighbors, and historians, in order to elucidate and corroborate the myriad of factual evidence. I corresponded with scholars in Canada, the midwest, and Pennsylvania, all of whom provided much useful information. I visited the Archives of the Mennonite Church and the Mennonite Historical Library, both at Goshen College, and came away with an abundance of invaluable source material.

Given the extent of Hutterian history, writing an exhaustive account is virtually impossible. I hope this book will help the reader understand the Hutterite culture, while recounting the experiences of one particular community, the Spokane Hutterian Brethren.

There are many persons whose assistance proved invaluable to my work, and I wish to convey my deep appreciation to all those who contributed their time. I am indebted to Paul S. Gross and his family for sharing so many of their experiences with me; indeed the entire membership of the Spokane Hutterian Brethren deserves acknowledgement for being the subject of this treatise. The Hutterites are a people worth knowing, and I am fortunate to have been allowed into their homes.

The initial stages of research were greatly assisted by Daniel T. Anderson at the *Spokesman-Review*, who located and collected all the local newspaper articles about the Hutterites. I received much encouragement and assistance from various faculty at Eastern Washington University: Dr. Michael Green who supported the project; Dr. Elwyn Lapoint who directed me toward the better literature regarding the Hutterites as a social group and who provided suggestions on ethnographic interviewing; and Mr. Richard Donley, who made the continued research possible with a travel grant to Goshen, Indiana.

I wish to thank Dr. Leonard Gross for his assistance in locating sources and his valuable suggestions, and his wife Irene for graciously welcoming me into their home and sharing her insights and opinions. The staff of the Archives of the Mennonite Church provided an open-door policy which enabled me to conduct research far into the night. Dr. John Roth directed me to the stacks of the Mennonite Historical Library where additional material was discovered, and Dr. John

Hostetler contributed solid ideas and suggestions towards successful research.

I would like to recognize the Stewart Book Scholarship Committee of Eastern Washington University for awarding me the *Chronicle of the Hutterian Brethren*, a primary document of epic proportions. My thanks to Dr. J. William T. Youngs, whose technical direction was invaluable during the entire investigation, and to Ms. Gretchen George, who committed many hours to typing the manuscript, transforming a stack of paperwork into a book. Finally, I wish to extend my deepest gratitude to my wife Kristin, on whose unfailing support I continually relied, and to my parents, who gave me constant encouragement.

# THE PLOUGH AND THE PEN
## PAUL S. GROSS AND THE ESTABLISHMENT OF
## THE SPOKANE HUTTERIAN BRETHREN

# *Chapter 1*
# INTRODUCTION

Although the Reformation brought an end to the long hegemony of the Roman Catholic Church in Europe, and subsequently much of the world, the Protestant and Reformed Churches continued to maintain the Roman-Catholic-style alliance between church and state. Numerous scholars and theologians considered the reforms cosmetic at best. To them, the Protestant Reformation did not advance far enough, so, not long after Martin Luther initiated the Reformation, the Radical Reformation took place.

It began in Switzerland and soon spread throughout Europe. Followers of this highly sectarian movement chose to abandon the established churches. They insisted that true New Testament reformation must result in communities of believers who practiced the literal tenets of the Bible. They rejected government control of their spiritual lives, refused to bear arms, and would not swear allegiance to any political body.

The most visible group was labeled Anabaptist. This derogatory term means "re-baptizer." Anabaptists, after careful scrutiny of the Scriptures, decided that infant baptism had no biblical basis. Baptism, therefore, was to be received only as an adult, and only after achieving an understanding of the Christian faith. At the time of baptism, the communicant made a public confession of faith. This essential creed of the Anabaptists was considered a heretical defiance of the established church. Moreover, since church and state were virtually synonymous, the nonconformist views held by the Anabaptists were threatening to the established social order.

So the Anabaptists were ruthlessly persecuted. Thousands of people were imprisoned, tortured, and/or executed for their faith. Others fled, migrating to the far reaches of the Holy Roman Empire, where religious tolerance existed in varying degrees. Still others remained in their homelands and continued to practice their faith secretly. Although both secular and religious establishments persecuted the Anabaptists, and suppressed the movement in many areas, they could not eradicate it.

In 1528 a group of Austrian Anabaptists, led by Jacob Widemann, left Nickolsburg, in Moravia (part of the modern Czech Republic), to escape the disdain of their neighbors, who advocated bearing arms. On this journey a significant event took place. Following the example of the early apostolic community in Jerusalem, the leaders of the group spread a cloak on the ground, and everyone deposited his or her personal possessions on it. The goods were then used or distributed as the need arose. Thus began the practice of "community of goods." This group settled in Austerlitz, also in Moravia, where they developed their system of Christian communal living.

These were the founders of the Hutterian Brethren, but they would not be known as such until after their bishop, Jacob Hutter, was martyred in 1536. Through the efforts of Jacob Hutter and his assistants, a well-defined communal pattern of living was established which remains virtually unchanged today. Hutter's leadership was so effective and noteworthy that his name was used to describe the people he led.

The Hutterian Brethren experienced "golden years" while in Moravia. Feudal nobles considered them excellent tenants, and provided protection for them in defiance of Hapsburg imperial dictates. Hutterian *bruderhofs* (houses of the brethren) thrived, and attracted thousands of members. By 1620, however, the power of the nobility was broken by the Thirty Years War, and the Hutterites were forced to flee. They migrated first to Hungary and then to Transylvania and Wallachia (both in modern Romania).

During the following 150 year period, the Hutterian Brethren suffered severely from the Roman Catholic Church's attempts to reconvert them. Many Hutterites abandoned their faith. Thousands, however, refused and were imprisoned or executed. Relentless persecution made

# Introduction

communal living impossible and it was abandoned. Only when a group of Carinthian Lutherans from Austria was deported to Romania and merged with the Hutterites was "community of goods" reestablished. This group of people fell victim to the ravages of war between Russia and the Ottoman Empire. Many people were killed or taken captive. Those that remained were invited by a Russian count to settle on his estate in the Ukraine. The Hutterites accepted his offer, and in 1770 the remnants of the Hutterian Brethren arrived in Vishenka. Here they were assured religious freedom and exemption from military service.

The tolerant regime of Catherine the Great, however, gave way to more militaristic rule, and in 1871 the Hutterites lost their right to freedom from conscription. Rather than give up this privilege, and thus compromise their principles, they decided once again to emigrate, this time to the United States. The migration came in three waves: the first Hutterites arriving in 1874, the last in 1879.

Through the centuries, only three groups of Anabaptists have endured: the many varieties of Mennonites, now spread throughout the U.S. and the world; the Amish, who live in the United States; and the Hutterian Brethren of the United States and Canada, who have in recent times also established splinter communities in England, Japan and Nigeria.

While virtually all Anabaptists agree about religious convictions, the distinguishing mark of the Hutterites has always been their practice of "community of goods." It is this custom which sets them apart in Christian society.

*Chapter 2*

# THE SOCIETY

Familiarity with contemporary Hutterian culture is helpful in understanding Hutterian history. The following is a brief overview of Hutterian life today.

Hutterites live in communes of up to 150 people. They usually practice dry-land agriculture on a large scale.[1] A Hutterian colony[2] strives to be a completely self-sufficient unit. The Hutterites raise virtually everything they need for their sustenance, and only buy what they cannot produce on their land. Items on a shopping list might include coffee, tea, sugar, salt, light bulbs, or chemicals. They use the most modern technology available to conduct extremely successful farming operations. The Hutterites are astute business administrators, and their colonies are usually relatively wealthy. When a colony's population reaches its limit, it uses its assets to "branch," to generate a daughter colony. This critical point varies, depending on the colony and the types of work it does.

When a colony "branches," half of the population departs to a pre-selected site, taking its share of the assets with it. The new colony then proceeds to regenerate, as does the parent colony.

Continuous growth has given the Hutterites in North America a population of about 40,000 people living in approximately 400 colonies.[3] The Hutterian Brethren double their population every seventeen years, more or less.[4] This phenomenon, combined with the unusual way they dress, has at times led mainstream American society to ostracize them.

Each Hutterite colony is a religious as well as an economic community. The backbone of Hutterian culture is religious; the colony itself is viewed as a biblical tenet.

> Hutterites sometimes compare the colony to the ark of
> Noah in the biblical account of the flood. Only those in
> the ark (the colony) are prepared to escape the judge-
> ment of God and to receive eternal life. In the Hutterite
> view, "You either are in the ark, or you are *not* in the
> ark."[5]

As the center of the Hutterite's universe, the colony is, of necessity, an orderly operation. The hierarchy in the community, thought to be divinely ordained, gives older people authority over younger, men authority over women, and the colony authority over individual members. The word of God is the ultimate authority over the commu-nity. In this hierarchy there is no room for compromise.[6]

The fundamental principle on which Hutterianism is founded is the importance of baptism.

> Baptized members are believed to have received the
> supernatural gift of the Holy Spirit through obedience
> and submission and to have more power and respon-
> sibility over those who have not been baptized.[7]

While this belief pertains to both men and women, it is the baptized men who regulate Hutterian life. The governing authority is a council of (male) elders.[8]

At the head of each community is the minister, the spiritual leader of the colony. The minister receives no formal training for his position. He is first elected to the post of assistant minister. After several years of probation wherein he proves his leadership capabilities, he is ordained by the bishop to the office of head minister. The head minister also has the role of secular leader, which involves him in virtually every aspect of the colony's life.

> He disseminates information, interprets doctrine, settles
> disputes, administers punishment, keeps travel records,
> checks on council members, and otherwise acts as
> "shepherd of the flock."[9]

# Figure 1
## Organizational Structure of North American Hutterites

# MEN

## Governing Council
First Minister
Second Minister
Secretary/Treasurer
Farm Boss (supervises crops)
Other. (This may be Chicken man,
German teacher, or other department manager.
German teacher may supervise garden.)

## Departmental Managers
### Agricultural Area
Cow Boss, Pig Boss, Sheep Boss
Duck & Geese Boss, Crops, Garden
### Technical Area
Blacksmith, Carpenter, Mechanic, etc.

## Labor Force
All men 15 years of age & older.
(All men on governing council and those holding department
managers' roles are available for work in specific need areas.
Shifts are often made during harvest season, etc.)

# WOMEN

## Head Cook
Tendency toward being wife of one of the ministers.
May be wife of farm boss or secretary/treasurer.
(Only executive position for women; not elected.)

## Labor Force
All women.
(Women obtain semi-retired status at age 45.
Garden and kindergarten women rotate.)

NOTE: All adult males are part of the group decision-making body
called the assembly (women are not allowed).

Source: From a handout distributed by Lawrence Anderson, Mankato State University

The next man in the hierarchy of authority is the manager. The man in this important position oversees the entire business enterprise of the colony, including the financial administration. He consults frequently with the men who run the various individual operations. Also called the "householder" or the "boss," he might be anywhere at anytime. The householder manages all commercial transactions with the outside world, and distributes commodities to the individual operations and households as needed.[10] Since an agrarian enterprise requires continuous attention, he is a busy man indeed.

There is a man to run each individual aspect of community work. These may include the field boss, the machine shop boss, the woodshop boss, the dairy man, the sheep man, and so on. Beneath these foremen are the men and older boys who comprise the workforce. Daily tasks are assigned by each boss. The boys work as apprentices under the men.

Among the women there is only one official post, that of head cook. All the other women and older girls comprise the workforce assigned to perform traditional women's work.

Women take turns cooking, gardening, cleaning, and overseeing the kindergarten. They also make most of the clothing for the members of their own households. Most importantly to Hutterian culture, women are the bearers of children.

Hutterites do not change as rapidly as the rest of modern society. Any change must be formally approved by the council. Hutterites are quite wary of change and the possible negative effect it may have on their culture. Modifications which improve the community economically, such as a fully-loaded John Deere tractor, are eagerly sought. Personal conveniences, such as microwaves and dishwashers, are generally considered "worldly" and shunned.[11]

Children spend their days at home until they are about three years old, at which time they begin to spend most of each day in the kindergarten. This allows the mother to resume a full-time work schedule, and also teaches the child valuable social skills.

Hutterite children attend state (or province) approved schools, which are generally located on the colony grounds. A certified teacher from the outside is hired to guide them through a curriculum which is equivalent to an early-high-school education. This is deemed sufficient for Hutterian purposes. At fifteen years of age, the individual is considered an adult and enters the workforce.[12]

The work conducted in a Hutterite colony is intense and varies with the seasons. Hutterites receive no wages for their work.[13] However, they receive complete provision for their temporal needs throughout their entire lives.

Families live together, but once the day begins a separation takes place. At breakfast, and at all meals, children eat in a dining hall separate from the adults. People sit in a segregated fashion: men at one table, women at another. They sit in descending order by age, with the oldest person at one end of the table and the youngest at the other. Meals begin and end with prayer. The rest of the meal is usually silent, and is a fairly quick affair.[14] After breakfast, everyone goes to his or her assigned destination: children to kindergarten, school-age youth to their lessons, and the adults to their respective work assignments. They rejoin for the two subsequent meals, but are generally not together again as families until the work day is over.

All Hutterites are trilingual. Their primary language is an Austrian dialect known as *Huttrisch*. Their daily routine is conducted in this language, which is considerably different from High German, the language they use to address all things religious. This is their highest form of expression and is considered indispensable to their culture.[15] English is, of necessity, their third language, and is spoken when addressing "the world."[16]

Hutterian children learn Huttrisch first, at home. Upon reaching school age, the children attend the German school, where they are taught to read and write the language of their Bible. German school is conducted in the morning and afternoon, before and after the regular school session. They are, of course, taught their regular curriculum in English. Thus Hutterites possess a wide range of forms of expression, which adds to the color of their lives.

The Hutterian Brethren are quaintly picturesque in their appearance. Their prescribed clothing and grooming serve as identity symbols which distinguish them from the rest of the world. The men all dress alike, as do the women. This uniformity of appearance diminishes the notion of individual pride in oneself and advances the idea of a united front.

Hutterian men wear dark denim trousers and jackets. Plaid shirts, often bright ones, are worn for working, and white shirts are worn for religious gatherings. Suspenders are used instead of belts. Beards are mandatory after marriage, especially after the first child is born, but both hair and beards are kept fairly short.[17] Hats are a usual addition to the men's costume. These may be of either light straw or dark material, or, in some cases, common billed "ball caps." A black felt hat, much like a large derby, is worn to religious gatherings, but is removed once inside.

The women make a greater visual impact than the men do. They always wear ankle-length dresses and long aprons reminiscent of their central European heritage. Patterns are allowed, either plaids or floral prints. A black kerchief with white polka dots is usually the prescribed head covering, and is always worn outside. On occasion it is pushed back or removed while indoors,[18] but it is always worn at religious gatherings.

Under a woman's head scarf is her long hair, which is almost never cut throughout her life. Naturally, this can result in hair that often reaches the ground. To counter this potential hindrance to work, and in accord with tradition, the back part of the hair is braided, either singly or doubly, and rolled into a bun which is held in place by a hairpin. The sides are then combed, turned under, brought back, and rolled around the bun.[19]

Infants are often brightly clothed. Small boys usually dress in overalls, evoking the suspenders worn by older males. When children reach school age, or somewhere thereabouts, they begin to dress exactly like adults: boys in dark trousers with suspenders, and girls in long dresses, aprons, and kerchiefs.

Adornments on the body, such as rings, necklaces, and earrings, are considered haughty items of "the world" and are discouraged. Watches are sometimes a necessity during working hours, a pocket watch being preferable to a wristwatch. Homes are also sparsely decorated. Clocks and calendars are accepted, as are small drawings or other crafts made by the Hutterites themselves.

The Hutterites are colorful in their simplicity. Their practices often vary from colony to colony, and always at the discretion of the council. The uniformity of Hutterite life encourages the peacefulness they experience in their communities. Theirs is a collective life filled with hard work, a life of devotion, in which personal contacts and familial relations are close and enduring.

Hutterian society is a mystifying one, and the preceding account is only a cursory introduction. The intricacies of Hutterian life are legion, and one could spend a lifetime studying them. John Bennett, a noted sociologist, explains:

> In spite of their unity, however, they elude easy classification. They are an ethnic group, a culture, an economy, a sect, a branch of Christianity, and a kind of "nation." They are, in short, a unique people; a people from whom there is much to be learned . . .[20]

# NOTES

1. Some communities engage in the manufacturing of farm implements, machinery or toys for handicapped children.

2. As citizens of the United States and Canada, some Hutterites consider the term "colony" to be inappropriate. Although it is generally accepted, for some people the term carries the connotation of foreigners who "do not belong." William (Bill) Gross, Manager, Spokane Hutterian Brethren, telephone interview with the author, October 20, 1991.

3. See John Hostetler, *Hutterite Society*, (Baltimore: The Johns Hopkins University Press, 1974), 290-293.

4.    William Kephart, *Extraordinary Groups*, (New York: St. Martin's Press, 1976), 272.

5.    Hostetler, *Hutterite Society*, 153.

6.    John Hostetler, *Communitarian Societies*, (New York: Holt, Rinehart & Winston, Inc., 1974), 36.

7.    Hostetler, *Hutterite Society*, 162.

8.    Hostetler, *Hutterite Society*, 162.

9.    Kephart, *Extraordinary Groups*, 250.

10.   Kephart, *Extraordinary Groups*, 250.

11.   There are varying degrees of acceptable change amongst the colonies. It is largely a matter of council approval. As a general rule, a change that would alter the basic framework of Hutterian identity is forbidden.

12.   The limitation of Hutterian formal education meets state and provincial requirements. For a comprehensive treatise on Hutterian education, see John Hostetler, "Total Socialization: Modern Hutterite Educational Practices," *Mennonite Quarterly Review*, XLIV (January 1970) 72-84.

13.   Small allowances are usually approved for the occasional trip to town and are administered by the manager.

14.   The minister and the very old eat in their homes.

15.   Hostetler, *Hutterite Society*, 149.

16.   Given their heritage, and the fact that English is the third language to be learned, Hutterites possess a marked "German accent."

17.   This is in contrast to Amish men, who have characteristically long hair and beards.

18.   This is the author's personal observation, experienced only after a lengthy and acknowledged rapprochement.

19.   Small girls are similarly groomed, but instead of turning the front hair under, it too is braided and pulled back.

20.   John W. Bennett, *Hutterian Brethren*, (Stanford, Stanford University Press, 1967), 52.

*Chapter 3*

# RECENT HISTORY

## The Leute

Up to 1874, the Hutterian Brethren were a single entity, all descending from the original group founded in 1528. In the process of migrating to North America, they became three distinct groups. Though the three groups are a phenomenon of their American experience, their origins are in Russia.

The Hutterites who migrated to the Ukraine in the 1770s were a group of only about sixty people.[1] By 1819 there was disunity among the ministers, as well as a spiritual decline among the Brethren as a whole, most likely due to their small and troubled population. They abandoned "community of goods" for the second time in their history. Their spiritual fire, however, did not die completely. "The brothers and sisters held together as congregations, faithfully reading the old Hutterian writings."[2] The Hutterites petitioned the Russian Crown to allow them to move to the south. By 1842 the entire group had relocated in the Molotschna District of the Ukraine. There were many German-speaking Mennonites in this region, who helped them acquire land on which to farm.[3] Upon their arrival in the Molotschna District, the Hutterites established five settlements: Huttertal, Johannesruh, Hutterdorf, Nau-Huttertal, and Scheromet. In these villages, patterned after the Mennonite villages, the dwellings faced a large street which ran through the community. Orchards and fields stretched out behind the homes. Over time, these villages grew and became virtually indistinguishable from the surrounding villages. In an attempt to assimilate into the greater Mennonite population, young Hutterian men and women apprenticed on Mennonite farms.[4] Initially the Hutterites and the Mennonites used their parallel experiences and similar creeds to establish a bond. However, differences in dress, speech, values, and practices all worked against rapprochement.[5] Moreover, the Hutterites maintained their own elected ministers, and worshipped separately from the Mennonites.[6] "The threat of being assimilated by the Mennonites . . . and the task of maintaining a separate identity were factors which contributed to the renewal of communal living."[7]

Various attempts to reestablish this, their central tenet, were made, and finally, in 1859, Reverend Michael Waldner succeeded in establishing a bruderhof of seventeen families at the far reaches of the village of Hutterdorf.[8] Waldner had been a blacksmith, and his followers were called *Schmiedeleut*, meaning "the people of the blacksmith."[9] It was the Schmiedeleut, under Michael Waldner's leadership, who were the first immigrants to America, in 1874. Upon their arrival in the Dakota Territory, this group purchased a 2,500 acre ranch near Tabor, South Dakota, "for the extortionate price of $25,000."[10] The Schmiedeleut named their bruderhof Bon Homme, and embarked on a life of full "community of goods." All of the colonies which recognize Bon Homme as their mother colony are known as Schmiedeleut communities; presently they are found only in South Dakota and Manitoba.

Waldner's original bruderhof, founded in Hutterdorf, ". . . turned out to be a significant success . . ."[11] A year later another elder, Darius Walter, followed suit with roughly the same number of families.[12] Interestingly, the bruderhof he established was located at the other end of Hutterdorf.[13] These people, the *Dariusleut*, were the second group to immigrate to America.

> The second group moved to Silver Lake, and like the
> Bon Homme people, spent the very severe first Dakota
> winter in sod huts. In the spring they bought 5400 acres
> on the James River, a tributary of the Missouri.[14]

Wolf Creek Colony, located near Freeman, South Dakota, was the mother colony of the Dariusleut bruderhofs. Today, the Dariusleut are found in Washington, Montana, Alberta, and Saskatchewan.

The Hutterites who remained in the Ukraine soon decided to follow their brethren to America.[15] The leader of one group was a highly educated and devout preacher named Jacob Wipf. He had unsuccess-fully attempted to form a bruderhof while still in the Ukraine. In 1877 Jacob Wipf established a bruderhof near Parkston, South Dakota, naming it Old Elm Spring.[16] Wipf was a teacher, which in German is *lehrer*. Thus, Old Elm Spring was the mother colony of the *Lehrerleut* colonies in America. They now are spread throughout Montana, Alberta, and Saskatchewan.

Through the course of the Hutterian experience in America, these three *leute* (literally "peoples") have adopted practices which differ only slightly from one another. Even though there are variations of dress, colony regulations, method of electing officers, and diet, they are essentially a single body with respect to their faith and principles. Their common religious literature ensures no deviation from their fun-damental tenets.[17]

During the early years in America, there was considerable intermar-riage among the three groups. As the number of daughter colonies in each group increased, this practice gradually decreased; today it is virtually nonexistent. A Dariusleut girl in a Montana colony was once asked if she would consider marrying outside her kinship group. She replied: "Never! Why, they dress so funny! I'd just as soon not get married."[18]

Some scholars suggest that the Lehrerleut are more conservative because they adopted communal living only after their arrival in Dakota. While they are, in fact, the most conservative of the three groups, there is no evidence that this is the result of their late return to "community of goods."[19] Subtle differences aside, the Schmiedeleut, the Dariusleut, and the Lehrerleut are all ethnic descendants of the same Anabaptist movement of the 1500s.

Over 1,200 people of Hutterian heritage migrated from the Ukraine to America. Of these, approximately 800 were incorporated into the three bruderhofs in Dakota. The remainder chose to live as individual family units, taking advantage of the Homestead Act of 1862.

"These non-colony Hutterites did not settle along the Missouri or James Rivers, but instead chose land available on the prairie."[20] These people were dubbed *Prairieleut* by their communal counterparts.

Though there was some interaction between them and the bruderhofs during the first years in America, the Prairieleut were soon absorbed into the larger society, and eventually became affiliated with the Mennonites of the region.[21]

There are several other groups which are labeled Hutterian Brethren. In 1920, a man named Eberhard Arnold led a small movement in Germany which adopted communal living. This group was called The Society of Brothers.

> The new community, founded on the Sermon on the Mount and formed in the spirit of the early church, attracted many who were looking for a new society to end war and its evil consequences.[22]

Arnold had read the history of the Anabaptist movements and wanted in particular to emulate the Hutterian ideal of "community of goods". He did not, however, know that the Hutterites were alive and well, for they seemed to have disappeared from the history books. Shortly after World War I, Arnold read of two Hutterites who had died in an American prison in 1918. He finally established communication with the Hutterites after 1926.[23] His exchange of letters with Elias Walter of Stand Off Colony in Alberta led to an invitation for Arnold to visit the bruderhofs in America. He visited all thirty-three Hutterite colonies in 1930 and 1931.

> He found that the brothers, after four hundred years, were still united in their basic faith and trust in God and in their practice of adult baptism; they shared their goods, work, and life; they made a commitment to the church as the body of Christ; they promised life-long faithfulness in marriage; they exercised church discipline; and they were united – to the last member – in their refusal to do military service.[24]

Eberhard Arnold was convinced that his group of believers should merge with the Hutterites. The Hutterites in turn deemed him sincere and worthy; he was ordained by Elias Walter in 1930. Arnold returned to Germany and established the Rhön bruderhof. He died in 1935.[25]

The rise of German National Socialism proved detrimental to the *Arnoldleut*. The Gestapo dissolved the bruderhof, which numbered over one hundred people, in 1937. Consequently, the Arnoldleut were forced to flee their homeland, an experience common to Hutterianism. They relocated in England for a time, but under pressure from the government, "which feared the group would aid the Germans in a possible invasion,"[26] moved to Paraguay by 1941. In the early 1950s, the Arnoldleut moved to the United States, first to North Dakota, and later to Pennsylvania. Subsequent colonies were established, in New York in 1954, in Connecticut in 1956, and in England in 1972.[27]

Another group was formed by a Hungarian named Julius Kubbasek in the early 1930s. The *Juliusleut* attempted to integrate with the Alberta Hutterites but they never enjoyed a successful rapport. The Juliusleut moved to Bright, Ontario, and established their own bruderhof in 1941, where they practiced their own form of Hutterianism.[28]

Still another group of Hutterites exists in Japan. The Christian Community of New Hutterian Brethren, Owa Colony, was established in the 1970s. Their minister, Izomi Izeki, was ordained by the elders of the Hutterian Brethren in America.[29]

Finally, there is one other community worthy of note. The Fan Lake Brethren, in Elk, Washington, was established as a bruderhof, by Don Murphy (not an ethnic Hutterite), in July, 1990.[30] They own a small ranch of 180 acres, which supports a modest beef cattle operation, as well as a commercial gardening enterprise. Their main occupation, however, is computer-aided drafting and their company name is Applied Computing Services. According to their Articles of Incorporation, they

> . . . operate exclusively as a church for religious, benevolent, provident, educational purposes in accordance with the teachings and traditions of the Hutterian Brethren Church . . .[31]

Clearly the legacy of Jacob Hutter's organizational leadership, combined with the ideal of Christian communal living, is a continuing dynamic in the world. It has had a rich history of both persecution and accomplishment.

# Paul Gross – The Early Years

At various points throughout Hutterian history, often during times when they seemed to be needed the most, notable leaders have emerged. Many individuals have helped set the course of Hutterian history and policy, by virtue of their strong leadership capabilities and their deep commitment to Hutterian principles. In the 20th century, a period of rapid growth and change, one leader who has figured prominently is Paul S. Gross.

Paul Gross was born at Wolf Creek on a winter's day, January 15, 1910.[32] The Hutterites use physicians, and Mrs. Mary Gross was assisted in childbirth by the local doctor.[33] At the time of Paul's birth, the Dariusleut had been farming the southeast corner of South Dakota for only thirty-five years. The colonies along the James River had flourished with the passing of just one generation.

Paul's father, Fred Gross, had been born in America, one of the first generation of United States Hutterites. He was the mason for the colony. The birth of a son in the harsh Dakota winter was cause for great joy, especially since Paul was the third son in the family.[34]

Throughout the remainder of the 1910 winter and into the spring, the infant Paul, like all Hutterite babies, spent much of his time in the arms of his mother, being breast-fed, sung to, and prayed for.[35]

When Paul was two years old, part of Wolf Creek Colony branched and moved to the vicinity of Lewistown, Montana, to establish the Spring Creek Colony.[36] Here Paul first became aware of the structured lifestyle which characterizes Hutterian culture. At three years of age, no longer a "house child," he entered the *Kleinschule*, or "little school." This Hutterian version of kindergarten was developed in Moravia centuries before formal kindergarten was introduced to the world.[37] Its form has remained virtually unchanged, and it has always been here that Hutterite children begin their cultural indoctrination. Under the tutelage of an elderly matron, usually a grandmother, Paul and the other very young children learned "to obey, pray, and keep out of the way."[38] The children were introduced to their culture in Huttrisch; Paul would not be exposed to English until he was five or six.

When he reached this age, Paul entered the English grade school as a first grader, and progressed in his studies as normally expected. He also had assigned duties appropriate for his age. He often found himself cleaning the chicken barn, while other young children helped herd sheep, pluck goose feathers, watch over even younger children, or work in the garden.

> I lived in Montana for eight years. What I remember most are the timber wolves that used to come down from the hills to kill our sheep and our calves. A timber wolf seems mighty big when you're nine years old.[39]

## World War I

For a time, life proceeded uneventfully for young Paul and his community on the Montana plains, despite the timber wolves. Then the unexpected came. The Great War had raged for several years before the United States entered the hostilities. When American troops were finally mobilized, the country became fanatically patriotic. The Selective Service Act, passed by Congress in 1917, created the first, and perhaps the greatest, conflict between the Hutterian Brethren and the United States Government.

Men between the ages of twenty-one and thirty-one were subject to the draft; there were no provisions for conscientious objection to war. Those who did not freely join the cause were harassed, and pacifist peoples, such as the Hutterites and the Mennonites, were violently persecuted by the military and by the population at large.[40]

> Long before the first men were drafted, the colony leaders agreed among themselves that their men could register and report for their physical examinations, but when they arrived at the induction center, they should cooperate no further.[41]

This decision was reached in accordance with the Hutterian view toward military service of any kind: their men were not to bear arms or even to wear the uniforms of the armed forces.

The Hutterites, represented by David Hofer, Elias Walter, and Joseph Kleissasser, and assisted by John Horsch as mediator between them and the government, made a formal petition to the president, Woodrow Wilson, requesting provision for their stance toward military service. This document, showing the total humility of the Hutterian Brethren, is worthy of note:

> We, the Hutterian Brethren Church, also known as Bruderhof or Communistic Mennonites, comprising about 2000 souls, who are living in eighteen communities in South Dakota and Montana (organized as a Church since 1533) kindly appeal to you, Mr. President and your Assistants, briefly wishing to inform you of our principles and convictions regarding military service. Being men of lowly station and unversed in the ways of the world, we would ask your indulgence if in this letter we should miss the approved form . . .
>
> Dear Mr. President, we humbly ask that we may be permitted the liberty to live according to the dictates of our conscience as heretofore. With the vow of baptism we have promised God and the Church on bended knees to consecrate, give and devote ourselves, soul and body and all, to the Lord in heaven, to serve Him in the way which, according to His Word we conceive to be acceptable to him. We humbly petition our Honored Chief Executive that we may not be asked to become disobedient to Christ and His Church, being fully resolved, through the help and grace of God, to suffer affliction, or exile, as did our ancestors in the times of religious intolerance, rather than violate our conscience or convictions and be found guilty before our God.
>
> We desire to serve our country and be respectful and submissive in every way not interfering with serving our God consistently. We are sincerely thankful for having been granted shelter and protection by our government and for having enjoyed full religious freedom up to the present time, and are quite willing to do something for

the good of our country, providing that it is not against our conscientious convictions.[42]

This document shows that the Hutterian Brethren, though peaceful non-resisters, were willing to argue their views in debate with the world, in the hope of promoting their most basic tenet of love. The Hutterite's formal *Conscientious Objection to Military Service*, a separate document which is signed by all Hutterians, states, in part:

> The only measure authorized by Christ to deal with our enemies is love and benevolence. And in accordance with the above, our good Master has taught us to pray for our enemy, since we are not allowed to hate, for the attitude of hatred toward another is equivalent to the sin of murder . . . We remain free from political ambitions and recognize civil Government as ordained of God . . . It is our daily prayer that the country may stay in peace . . . As God permits, we further desire to serve our country as agriculturalists in ways and duties that do not interfere with our religious convictions.[43]

The text of this document incorporated many elements of the petition made to Woodrow Wilson in 1917.

In spite of the freedom of religion granted the citizenry of the United States in the Constitution, the Hutterian Brethren received no support from the government.

> Americans were as yet totally unprepared to comprehend sincere conscientious objection to war and consequently all conscientious objectors were dismissed as cowards.[44]

The only quasi-provision enacted was Wilson's establishment of non-combatant military status. In March, 1918, Wilson announced that the pacifists, Hutterites included, were expected to join the military " . . . in a non-combatant role."[45] This was still unacceptable to the Hutterites, for they considered this supporting the war effort.

When the Hutterite delegation of ministers went to Washington to petition President Wilson, they were only able to speak with Secretary of War Baker. He advised the Hutterian Brethren to simply let their men go to the training camps and to deal with their consciences.[46] The Hutterites had no recourse but to do just that.[47] Paul Gross was very young, but still remembers:

> Some of our people, they went to camp from Montana. My uncle, he was married already and he went to camp in Kansas – Camp Funston. He was a man from the Schmiedeleut and he married my aunt and came to live with his wife in Montana. There, they took him away, took him to camp. He also had a few children already; it was a sad time.[48]

It was a sad time indeed, but it was not surprising. The Hutterites had borne persecutions of this nature throughout their history. During the persecutions of the Catholic Reformation, the Anabaptists met their deaths with joy and singing. They considered the suffering of injustice as central to true Christian discipleship, and they came to expect to be persecuted.

To the Hutterites, names such as Funston, Lewis, Dodge, Alcatraz, and Leavenworth are synonymous with hateful persecution, and they have found their permanent places in Hutterite history. The diaries written in these camps, as well as the memoirs written and dictated in subsequent years by those who survived, chronicle the experiences endured by the Hutterites, as well as other conscientious objectors.[49]

One such man, Reverend Andrew Wurtz of the Lehrerleut, recalled his ordeal in a dictated memoir to his son, Andrew A. Wurtz.[50] He told of leaving Old Elm, the colony where he lived, and traveling to Parkston, South Dakota to board a train bound for Fort Lewis, in the State of Washington. On this train he was grouped with four other Lehrerleut Hutterians from Rockport Colony: Joseph, Michael, and David Hofer, and Jacob Wipf.

The men, already sensing the antagonism toward them, used a 2" x 4" wooden beam to barricade the door to their compartment. When they opened the door to speak with a lawyer whom they knew, a Mr. Damfer, who was also going to the camp, a number of other men stormed the compartment and assaulted the Hutterites. They forcefully cut Michael Hofer's and Jacob Wipf's hair and beards and they beat all five men. Though the conductor brought the melee to a halt, and there were no further incidents, the Hutterites remained afraid for the rest of the two days and night of the journey.

On reaching Fort Lewis, the Rockport Hutterites and Andrew Wurtz were separated, ". . . because I was with a different group."[51] Wurtz's hair and beard were cut, and the following morning he was ordered to march in formation. He refused. Thus began the ordeal he would face during most of his stay in the camp. He was forcibly stripped of his clothing and was roughly placed in a military uniform. He was forced to sign a paper "which allowed me to work in the hospitals."[52] He was ordered to pick up refuse in the hospital and to stoke the furnace. Wurtz refused both orders on the grounds that they would be aiding the war effort. When he dropped an armload of wood to the floor, accidently tearing Sergeant Dayley's uniform, the enraged sergeant ordered buckets of cold water poured over Wurtz's back and kicked him violently, "saying that his uniform was worth more than I was."[53]

Instances of abuse such as this were legion. Among other torments, Wurtz had wooden beams placed on his neck while he was lying on the ground, and he was forced to stand dangerously close to the blistering furnace which he had refused to fuel.[54]

During one ten-day period, which the Hutterites were allowed to spend together, they were fed only bread and water. Upon Wurtz's return to the Military Police Ward, Sergeant Dayley commanded him to polish the floor of the barracks. "The floor was constructed of soft wood and slivers were protruding from the floor."[55] When Wurtz refused this order, again claiming that he could not assist in activities that aided the war effort, Dayley ordered ropes tied to his legs and the ropes pulled, one leg at a time, while Wurtz held the floor polisher handle, thus forcing him to engage in a war-effort activity.

> Suddenly, they pulled both ropes, causing me to fall backwards, hurting my back and head and rendering me unconscious. They pulled me along the floor, up and down the hallway over the door ledges. I uttered an outcry – the slivers from the floor had penetrated my entire body. (I had only a light T-shirt and pyjamas on.)[56]

Wurtz was often given cold water "treatments"; at times he was held underwater in a filled bathtub to the point of near drowning, and other times he was placed under a cold shower tap for hours, with someone checking periodically to see that he had not turned on the warm water.[57] The Hutterian tenet of non-resistance did not allow Wurtz to alleviate his situation, in this instance by turning on warm water, or by fighting his punishments in any way. The frequency of these water treatments increased. Before and/or during them, depending on the Sergeant's mood, Wurtz was punched repeatedly in the stomach until he was unconscious. A soldier once struck him on the head with a broom handle, "using such force that the handle splintered into three pieces."[58]

There were many periods during which Wurtz was starved for weeks at a time. "The odor from my stomach was so pungent that I myself could not tolerate the odor."[59] During these starvation periods he was often taunted with plates piled high with food. The sergeant would tell him that, to get the food, he would have to work.

Andrew Wurtz wrote many letters home. None was ever mailed, nor did he receive any letters, except one. Sergeant Dayley told him: "If you can identify who wrote this letter, you may have it, but if you cannot, you will not have it."[60] Wurtz claimed that he received the God-given inspiration to say "Jacob M. Hofer."[61] He was correct!

He secretly managed to post one letter to his home. Upon receiving it, the Hutterites in South Dakota forwarded it to the Conscientious Objector's Office in Washington, D.C. In this letter, Andrew Wurtz detailed every single abuse to which he had been subjected.

A delegation was sent to Fort Lewis, and a hearing was held. It was determined that Andrew Wurtz had been treated "most improperly." He encountered no further trouble. Twenty-six letters from his kinfolk, which had been withheld, were delivered to him. When the war ended, Wurtz was discharged from Fort Lewis and arrived home within a month. "I was filled with extreme happiness and thanks to God that he kept me and gave me strength in my hard ordeal."[62]

Andrew Wurtz lived to tell of his wartime experience; others were not so fortunate. The Hofers and Jacob Wipf experienced much the same treatment upon their arrival at Fort Lewis. They, however, refused to sign any papers, wear uniforms, or do any work. They were placed in prison cells for two months. After two months they were condemned by the War Court to thirty-seven years with seventeen years suspended. They were sentenced to serve their time at Alcatraz. Chained together by hands and feet, the four men were transported by rail to California, a journey of two days.

> At their arrival at the Alcatraz prison, their clothes were taken from them by force. They received the command to put on the uniform, which they refused as before. Then they were brought to the lower level of the prison, into dark, dirty, and stinking cells for solitary confinement.[63]

They were thrown the uniforms with the words: "If you don't conform you'll stay here 'till you give up the ghost like the four we carried out yesterday."[64]

Considering the cold, wet concrete of their cells, the men, clad only in their underwear, must have suffered greatly during that first week of solitary confinement. They received only half a glass of water to drink every twenty-four hours. During the last one and a half days of the week they had to stand in silence. "Their hands were tied together above their heads and fastened to the iron rods above."[65]

The Hutterites were then let out of solitary confinement for a day, but they did not receive any food until evening. The whole procedure was then repeated. Only on Sundays were they given an hour of exercise in the courtyard. They endured this routine for four months. They were so fiercely bitten by insects, and their arms were so swollen, that they could not get their jackets over them.[66]

In late November, 1918, the four men were transferred to Fort Leavenworth, in the State of Kansas. The trip by rail, which took them through Texas, lasted four days and five nights, during which time they were chained together, two by two.

> They arrived at 11:00 p.m. in Leavenworth and were driven through the street like pigs, with much noise and the use of bayonets. Chained to each other's arms, they

carried in the other hand their bags and their bibles, and another pair of shoes under an arm. They were urged to hurry up the hill to the prison. By the time they reached the gate they were sweating so much that the hair on their heads was wet. In this condition, in the cold air, they had to take off their clothes in order to put on the prison dress which was brought to them. By the time this happened, about two hours later, at 1:00 a.m., they were frozen stiff. Early in the morning at 5 o'clock, they again had to stand in the cold air in front of a door and wait. Joseph and Michael Hofer could take it no longer; they had such a pain that they had to be taken to a hospital.[67]

Jacob Wipf and David Hofer were put into solitary confinement, where they had to stand for nine hours each day, chained to the bars of their cells. For fourteen days they were given only bread and water, then they received regular meals for another fourteen days, and so on, one regimen alternating with the other.[68]

Joseph and Michael Hofer were critically ill in the hospital. Jacob Wipf sent a telegram to their wives in South Dakota, who left Rockport Colony immediately.

Things were made worse because the railroad agent told them that the telegram had come from Fort Riley, [also in Kansas] and not from Fort Leavenworth. He sold them tickets to the wrong station and thus they lost a whole day. Finally they reached Fort Leavenworth and found their spouses dying, hardly able to speak.[69]

Joseph Hofer died during the night and was placed in a casket. The military ordered that he could not be viewed any more. His wife, Maria, pleaded for permission to see her husband one final time. This request was granted.

But to her horror she had to see that her beloved husband had been put into a uniform, which he in life had resisted so steadfastly in order to remain faithful to his convictions.[70]

Michael Hofer died a few days later. The military released the bodies, which were shipped to South Dakota accompanied by the relatives who had come to Fort Leavenworth. The attendance at the funerals of Joseph and Michael Hofer was enormous. Their martyrdom bolstered the religious convictions of many, and ". . . seared Hutterite minds with the price of true apostolic faith."[71]

David Hofer was released the following day. On January 27, 1919, by the order of the Secretary of War, 113 other conscientious objectors were released from Leavenworth. Jacob Wipf, however, was not among them. He was held until April 13th, and there were others who were held even longer.[72]

> The case of these four Hutterite brethren is one of exceptional severity . . . If anyone can call these men cowards he may do so. At least they are a living monument of what harmless religious men in this enlightened age have to suffer because their convictions don't agree with those of the rest of society.[73]

Hutterites in their home colonies also suffered abuses from the overzealous population. Many Americans regarded them with suspicion; after all, they were Germans, were they not? America at this time failed to acknowledge that she was a nation populated by immigrants, many of whom spoke languages other than English.

> What people could not realize, owing to the hysteria of war, was that the Hutterites deliberately retained German to insulate themselves from North American culture.[74]

Vicious rumors about the Hutterites spread throughout the Plains, such as that they were salting ground glass into the flour they milled for public sale and that they were actually helping the enemy by acts of internal espionage.[75] Such misunderstandings brought much suffering to the bruderhofs. Livestock was stolen from the colonies and sold at ridiculously low prices, and the money invested in war bonds.[76] The Hutterites, of course, refused to buy Liberty Bonds or to pay any form of war taxes.

Other incidents resulted in the physical abuse of some of the elders. Mennonite churches were painted yellow. Young men were forced to kiss the American flag, and, under the sanction of the Prohibition Act, the Hutterian wine supplies were confiscated. "The confiscated wine was distributed at the county seat [Yankton, South Dakota] in an Armistice Day Parade."[77]

The Hutterites meekly succumbed to all these activities on the American "home front." They did not, however, remain idle.

# NOTES

1. John Hostetler, *Hutterite Society*, (Baltimore: The Johns Hopkins University Press, 1974), 92.

2. *The Chronicle of the Hutterian Brethren*, (Rifton, NY: Plough Publishing House, 1987), 806.

3. This region lies approximately five hundred miles to the south of Vishenka and Radichev where the Hutterites had lived up to 1842.

4. Hostetler, *Hutterite Society*, 105.

5. Hostetler, *Hutterite Society*, 105.

6. Hostetler, *Hutterite Society*, 107.

7. Hostetler, *Hutterite Society*, 107.

8. Hostetler, *Hutterite Society*, 111. Hostetler discusses the great mystical and spiritual awakening which resulted in the reestablishment of communal living. It is important to note this Hutterian mysticism, and greater details are found in *Hutterite Society*, 110-112.

9. Paul Gross, *The Hutterite Way*, (Saskatoon: Freeman Publishing Company, 1965), 110.

10. Hostetler, *Hutterite Society*, 121.

11.     Gross, *The Hutterite Way*, 110. The Hutterites consider this spiritual awakening as being one of the most significant events in their history. Without community of goods, a characteristic unique to them, their identity as Hutterian Brethren may have been lost forever.

12.     Gross, *The Hutterite Way*, 110.

13.     Hostetler, *Hutterite Society*, 111. The importance of this second establishment is worthy of note; between the two bruderhofs there remained numerous individual households which were dependent on the Mennonites. Hostetler further notes: "In 1869 [the Schmiedeleut] moved to *Scheromet*, about eight and one-half miles away, where they were joined by others from *Johannesruh*." Ibid.

14.     Lawrence C. Anderson, "The Hutterian Brethren: With Emphasis on the South Dakota Schmiedeleut" (unpublished paper, 12th Annual Dakota History Conference, April 12, 1980), 5, 8.

15.     The migration to America was complete by 1879. All of the Hutterites who crossed the ocean, along with many of the Mennonites, settled in the Dakota Territory.

16.     Gross, *The Hutterite Way*, 111.

17.     Gross, *The Hutterite Way*, 112. To the untrained outsider, Hutterites often "look the same." Indeed, in many respects they do. Lehrerleut women, however, have larger polka dots on their kerchiefs than do the Dariusleut; Schmiedeleut women often wear light, white organdy bonnets similar to the Amish and the conservative Mennonites. Lehrerleut women make their dresses out of brighter patterns than the Dariusleut, who wear the darkest clothing. There are other examples of differences amongst the groups, including the forbiddance of toys in the Lehrerleut *Kleinschule*, while the other two groups permit some. Schmiedeleut children attend the *Kleinschule* until just before dinner at 6:00 p.m., while Lehrerleut children attend until 2:30. The subtle variations among the three groups are legion. For authoritative discussions regarding the leute, see John Hostetler, *Hutterite Society* and Karl Peter, *The Dynamics of Hutterite*

*Society* (Edmonton, Alberta: The University of Alberta Press, 1987).

18. William A. Allard, "The Hutterites, Plain People of the West," *National Geographic*, 138 (July, 1970) 112.

19. John Bennett, *Hutterian Brethren* (Stanford: Stanford University Press. 1967), 31. The varying degrees of Hutterian orthodoxy are mysterious dynamics, although the personal characteristics of the founders of the three groups may have some bearing.

20. Anderson, "The Hutterian Brethren," 8.

21. Gross, *The Hutterite Way*, 111-112. Most of these Prairieleut joined the Krimmer Mennonite Church, (named for the Crimea whence they emigrated), yet still consider themselves Hutterian by virtue of their heritage.

22. *Chronicle*, 807.

23. Arnold was able to establish communications with the Hutterian Brethren through Dr. Robert Friedmann of Vienna, a noted Anabaptist scholar.

24. *Chronicle*, 808.

25. *Chronicle*, 808.

26. Hostetler, *Hutterite Society*, 280.

27. The Arnoldleut and the ethnic Hutterites have experienced strained relations in the last forty years. The history of the schism is voluminous. For a concise discussion, see Hostetler, *Hutterite Society*, 280-283. The factors involved include the permissiveness within the Arnoldleut toward smoking, radios, television and movies, dancing, and such other things as not folding hands during prayer and "singing" the grace before meals. The Arnoldleut have published many works of Hutterian literature. As this book addresses the ethnic Hutterites, much of the Arnoldleut literature is omitted from the bibliography, except those works which the author considered imperative. The translation of the paramount primary source for early Hutterian history, *The Chronicle of the Hutterian Brethren*, for example, is a publication of the "Eastern Hutterites." The translated edition of Peter Ridemann's *Confession of Faith* (London:

Hodder & Stoughton; Rifton, NY: Plough Publishing House, 1950) used in this book is another work of the Arnoldleut; it was translated from the German by Kathleen Hasenberg of the *Sociedad Fraternal Huteriana*, in Paraguay.

28.  Hostetler, *Hutterite Society*, 279. The Hutterites severed relations with the Juliusleut in 1950 "giving as their reason that Julius was too dictatorial and impulsive and noting also that he was an advocate of celibacy." Ibid. Nevertheless, the colony in Ontario has attracted numerous converts and has been prosperous.

29.  *Chronicle*, 809. The Owa community originated in a small movement in the 1950s. Their ideal was to form a community of Christians reflective of the second chapter of the Book of Acts in the New Testament – precisely the identical force behind the original Hutterite movement of 1528. Izeki visited some of the colonies in America, was ordained, and his community enjoys complete approval from its Dariusleut counterparts.

30.  Fan Lake Brethren are easily accessible for further information, as well as for visiting purposes. Their address and telephone are: Fan Lake Brethren, 2762 Allen Road West, Elk, WA 99009. Telephone: (509) 292-0502

31.  Article III – Purposes.

32.  Paul S. Gross, minister, Spokane Hutterian Brethren, personal interview with the author at his home, Spokane County, November 7, 1991.

33.  Paul S. Gross, interview with the author, November 7, 1991. "I've got a birth certificate. That means that my mother had a doctor. He would have been the doctor from Freeman, South Dakota."

34.  Paul S. Gross, interview with the author, November 15, 1991.

35.  This is a general practice. See Hostetler, *Hutterite Society*, 208, 210.

36.  Paul Gross, interview with the author, November 15, 1991. For more details on the establishment of the Spring Creek Colony, see page 38.

37. Robert Friedmann, "Hutterite Education," in Robert Friedmann, *Hutterite Studies*, (Goshen IN: Mennonite Historical Society, 1961), 139.

38. Hostetler, *Hutterite Society*, 212.

39. Paul S. Gross, interview with the author, November 7, 1991.

40. Paul S. Gross, interview with the author, November 23, 1991.

41. Hostetler, *Hutterite Society*, 126-127.

42. For a complete reprint of the petition, see Appendix E, page 114.

43. *A Conscientious Objection to Military Service of an Anabaptist Group, a Religious Incorporation Known as The Hutterian Brethren of North America* (Reprint – Hutterian Brethren, Lind, WA).

44. Hostetler, *Hutterite Society*, 128.

45. David Flint, *The Hutterites: A Study in Prejudice* (Toronto: Oxford University Press, 1975), 71.

46. Hostetler, *Hutterite Society*, 128.

47. Of the 554 "Mennonite" conscientious objectors, it is estimated that about fifty were Hutterites. Hostetler, *Hutterite Society*, 127.

48. Paul S. Gross, interview with the author, November 23, 1991.

49. It is important to note that the Espionage Act of 1917, and the Sedition Act of 1918 enabled the administration of Woodrow Wilson, "the peacemaker," to silence any and all criticism of the government's participation in the war, including activities on the home front.

50. Andrew A. Wurtz, *The Memoirs of Reverend Andrew Wurtz: World War I - 1918: As Told to His Son Andrew A. Wurtz* (Warner, ALTA: Sunny Site Colony, n.d.)

51. Wurtz, *Memoirs*, 2. The meaning of "different group" cannot be ascertained from the translation. All these men were conscientious objectors, but perhaps they were separated because they came from different colonies.

52. Wurtz, *Memoirs*, 2.

53. Wurtz, *Memoirs*, 3. Sergeant Dayley was the noncommissioned officer in charge of Wurtz for his entire stay at Fort Lewis.

54. Wurtz, *Memoirs*, 3.

55. Wurtz, *Memoirs*, 4.

56. Wurtz, *Memoirs*, 4.

57. Wurtz, *Memoirs*, 4.

58. Wurtz, *Memoirs*, 5.

59. Wurtz, *Memoirs*, 5.

60. Wurtz, *Memoirs*, 6.

61. Wurtz, *Memoirs*, 6.

62. Wurtz, *Memoirs*, 9.

63. Franz Wiebe, trans., *The Martyrdom of Joseph and Michael Hofer, 1918*, (Elkhart, IN: Associated Mennonite Biblical Seminaries, 1974), 1, in A.J.F. Zieglschmid, *Das Klein-Geschichtsbuch der Hutterischen Bruder*, (Philadelphia: Carl Schurz Foundation, 1947), 482-486.

64. Wiebe, *Martyrdom*, 1.

65. Wiebe, *Martyrdom*, 2.

66. Wiebe, *Martyrdom*, 2.

67. Wiebe, *Martyrdom*, 2.

68. Wiebe, *Martyrdom*, 2.

69. Wiebe, *Martyrdom*, 2-3.

70. Wiebe, *Martyrdom*, 2-3.

71. Hostetler, *Hutterite Society*, 130.

72. Wiebe, *Martyrdom*, 4.

73. Wiebe, *Martyrdom*, 4.

74. Flint, *The Hutterites*, 73.

75. Flint, *The Hutterites*, 73.

76. Hostetler, *Hutterite Society*, 130.

77. Hostetler, *Hutterite Society*, 130-131.

## Chapter 4
# PINCHER CREEK – THE PRELUDE

### Background

A direct consequence of World War I on twentieth-century Hutterianism was a mass migration to Canada. This occurred immediately
following the armistice in 1918.

> At this juncture they were invited by the Canadian
> government to settle in Alberta and Manitoba. Both the
> government and the Canadian Pacific Railroad were
> anxious to bring hard-working settlers to parts of Alber-
> ta and Manitoba that had hitherto remained empty
> because of lack of resources or unfavorable climate.[1]

With the assurance of freedom from military conscription, the
Hutterites accepted the offer. Within two years, all but three bruderhofs
had moved north.[2] It was particularly odd that the Canadian government promised the Hutterites freedom from military conscription, the
right to live communally, and the right to independent private schools,
because in 1917 it had passed the Wartime Elections Act which, among
other things, denied the right to vote to conscientious objectors and
recently naturalized Canadian citizens.[3]

> This bill disqualifies for the War Time Election those of
> alien enemy birth or other European birth and of alien
> mother tongue or native language, who have been
> naturalized since the thirty-first of March, 1902. It is
> further to be noted that whosoever is disqualified from
> voting by this measure is at the same time exempted
> from combatant service in the war.[4]

The Hutterites were just as misunderstood in Canada as they had been
in the United States. Amid an atmosphere of national self-conscious-

ness, slanderous stories were written about them in the newspapers. English-speaking Canadians were having difficulty facing the fact that there was not one uniform cultural identity throughout the country.[5] Nonetheless, the Hutterites migrated en masse. Fifteen colonies were founded in Canada in 1918, six by the Schmiedeleut in Manitoba, and five by the Dariusleut and four by the Lehrerleut in Alberta. By 1920, eleven of the fifteen colonies had sold their South Dakota lands.[6]

Paul Gross's family was not part of the Canadian migration. Before the war, Fred Gross had already taken half of Wolf Creek Colony from South Dakota and established Spring Creek Colony near Lewistown, Montana.[7] They had purchased the Spring Creek Ranch from its owner, Joe King, who had travelled to South Dakota specifically to offer this tract of land, and his other ranch, King Ranch, to the Dariusleut Hutterites. "Since the land was so rich and had plenty of good water, we accepted his offer."[8]

The move to Spring Creek was a move into increased isolation.

> We found ourselves outside of the circle of the Hutterite group at this point. The Spring Creek Colony was the first colony in the State of Montana and the first successful, permanent establishment outside of South Dakota.[9]

The Grosses lived in Montana from 1912 to 1920. By 1920, South Dakota was virtually devoid of Hutterian communities, due to the Canadian migration. Many of the bruderhofs which migrated left behind fully established and quite successful farms. Paul's family decided to return to South Dakota from Spring Creek.

> The reason was, it was isolation in Montana. The offer was so good to repopulate one of these colonies, so we did; after eight years we moved back to South Dakota.[10]

At this time, communication between the Hutterites who had fled to Canada and those who remained in the United States was reestablished. When Fred Gross heard of the good land to be found in the north, he made a couple of scouting trips to Canada.

> The colony in South Dakota split and half the colony moved to Canada in 1924. I was amongst them that moved to Lethbridge, Alberta.[11]

The ranch that Fred Gross bought in 1924 belonged to a millionaire named Felger who had "gone broke."[12] The Felger Farm was home to the Gross family for only two years.

> It was an early harvest and a dry fall in 1926 and the Hutterite colony in the Lethbridge district was planning to leave and migrate further west towards the foothills of the Rocky Mountains, where nights are cool and mountain rain showers are more frequent.[13]

Paul's family was somewhat of a maverick group; never before had Hutterian Brethren left the prairie. The Hutterites who came to America in the 1870s chose to settle in the Dakota Territory because the land was similar to the steppes of the Ukraine; those that emigrated north to Canada after World War I established colonies on prairie land that resembled that of South Dakota. No families had ever gone westward. Such independence of mind would appear again, in the life of Fred Gross's son, Paul.

The group contacted a real estate agent in Lethbridge who had several ranches on his list, some of which were located near Pincher Creek.

> In those trying years many ranchers and farmers were facing the vicissitudes of their holdings and had them listed for sale. Many of their dwellings had already been abandoned, and down-and-out farmers lived with friends and relatives in town or went on relief.[14]

The Hutterites discussed their options at length, and the colony's steering committee decided to visit one particular ranch, "which seemed to be a duel-purpose [sic] development of farming and ranching."[15] The land they were investigating lay four miles northwest of Pincher Creek, four miles southwest of Pincher Station, and seventy-five miles west of Lethbridge. A number of other farms and ranches in the area were up for sale and the Hutterites also visited several of these. "Nothing better was found then [sic] the ranch the agent had for sale; the farm of Pete Hanson, consisting of 3,030 acres, of which was 875 acres of pasture land."[16]

Hutterites prefer to establish their communities away from urban developments of any size. This is to minimize the effect of worldly temptations on the minds of easily-influenced youth. Gross's group was pleased that the nearest railroad station was four miles away, and they proceeded with negotiations to buy Pete Hanson's ranch.

Ed and Rose Peck, who had managed the Hanson farm for years, expressed their desire to buy it as well.[17] The Pecks, however, had little capital and had not made any payments to the owner. Pete Hanson considered this the opportune time to materialize a deal to his benefit, and turned the problem over to his attorneys, Thompson & Jackson of Pincher Creek. The firm of Thompson & Jackson considered the problem and determined that the Hutterites were the more promising party. They too had little cash, but possessed a considerable holding in the Felger Farm in Lethbridge.

The negotiations soon contained a new twist: John Sandgren, Hanson's senior partner in their construction business, added his holdings, the Laughlin Bell Ranch and the Alberta Ranch, to the Hanson Ranch, with the proposal to trade it for the Hutterite's Felger Farm in Lethbridge. This acquisition comprised considerably more land than what they owned in Lethbridge. The Hutterites accepted the offer, taking on a substantial mortgage loan for payment to Pete Hanson, and ". . . the deals were negotiated, the move was in shape."[18]

The Hutterites now possessed a sizeable tract of land. The availability of an adequate water supply was, as always, crucial in deciding where to build the community. When a better supply was found a quarter of a mile southeast of the existing ranch house, "a crew was assigned to dig a well where a willow-twig witcher thought should be water, and surely some was found . . . Occasionally we had to haul water in barrels from Pincher Creek."[19] Thus, they decided to build new buildings a bit closer to Pincher Creek.

In the windy autumn of 1926, a work party from the colony in Lethbridge, together with carpenters from various other colonies, gathered to build the Pincher Creek bruderhof. Lumber was procured and shipped from Yates Lumber Company in Lethbridge, and work commenced on the chosen site.[20]

The building party, all men and boys, travelled from Lethbridge with a team of horses "pulling a large hay rack loaded with all kinds of provisions in which I was riding . . ."[21] The caravan proceeded across the Saint Mary River, through the Blood Indian Reserve, and reached Pincher Creek, stopping along the way for an overnight rest at Stand

Off Colony near Fort Macleod. While it is uncertain exactly how many days it took to travel from Felger to Pincher Creek, it must have been several. There was one notable incident on the trip:

> I still recall one of the hayrack wagons broke its axle right in the stoney bottum [sic] of the river. To get that fixed and going, everyone of the migration crew fell several times into the river and all were soaking wet.[22]

When they arrived, the men roomed in an old building on the Hanson site and immediately began pouring the concrete foundations.[23] This, the first task of building, was hurriedly completed before the late-autumn freeze.

> Building progress was made in a hurry, and after temporary arrangements the rest of the colony, women and children were coming by train, together with machinery and household goods.[24]

The colony then took shape fairly rapidly. Based on the typical Hutterian bruderhof building plan, most buildings faced inward toward the center of the community. At Pincher Creek, the machine shops and granaries were erected on the north side, the livestock barns on the east, living quarters on the west and the kitchen on the south, ". . . equal steps to be made for every one."[25] They utilized a vacant building for the school until, in later years, they built a new one.

Paul speaks kindly of the neighbors in the immediate vicinity of their new home. The local people showed much interest in these "new folk." During rare moments of spare time, visiting took place between the Hutterites and their neighbors. Among those whom Paul mentions in *Pincher Creek Colony: Memories* were the Pete Lehmans, who lived a mile to the east and "who were even so kind and let us use their telephone for out-going and in-coming calls."[26] Pete's son, Neil, lived to the northwest, and Ernest Connelly lived just across the highway. The Davidoffs, a Doukhobor family, owned a place just to the north of the colony, and Mrs. Dyck, a Mennonite widow also lived adjacent to the Pincher Creek bruderhof. There was also Jacob Meier, a bachelor from Germany, who resided to the southwest. "These were all wonderful neighbors."[27]

It must have been refreshing and pleasant for the Hutterian Brethren community at Pincher Creek to experience the kindness and assistance of these and other people. In view of the usual reception given to Hutterites, such treatment was miraculously rare indeed.[28]

## Changes and Developments

Between 1926 and the 1940s, agricultural technology changed dramatically. The farming practices of the Pincher Creek Hutterites also changed.

Traditionally, horses were central to the lives of the agrarian Hutterites. They needed many healthy, dependable animals for harvesting, as well as for numerous other farming tasks. Horses were also used for transportation, either ridden or hitched to buggies and wagons. In the words of Paul Gross:

> Cars and trucks were taboo for the Hutterites for many years to come. Going on long far trips, there were special buggies, prior to the rubber-tired Bennett buggy. Neighboring colonies were a distance of 30 to 50 miles, and to reach them you had to get up early and put a good day in. Visitors coming and going would stay a week and the horses would get a good rest.[29]

The horse trade directly linked the Hutterites in Pincher Creek with several of their neighbors. When the colony was first established, it was short of good work horses. Alfred Pelletier, a man who raised purebred bulls a few miles east of Pincher Creek, gave fifteen untamed horses to the colony for breaking.

> They had gotten old and out-of-hand. One of them, a huge sorrel, knocked my front teeth loose with his front feet, [they (the teeth)] eventually . . . had to be extracted. But somehow we tamed them and put them to work as long as he let us have them for breaking.[30]

They bought other horses from John Sandgren, a trusted friend of the Hutterites.

The horse gradually faded from the scene, as the Hutterites along with other farmers,  succumbed to mechanization.

> There was the Fred Robbins family, who operated a
> livery barn, . . . also maintaining the highway with a
> horse-drawn grader . . . He also had an acreage to farm
> south and west of Pincher Station. They were lover[s]
> of horses, and had good ones, . . . the last ones to give
> up and switch to tractors.[31]

The nostalgic photographs of yesteryear, showing combines, threshers,
and swathers attached to trains of horses, often numbering thirty or
more, show scenes that live in the memories of only the very old.
"Today's generation don't know anything about it. In fact, they would
not know how to harness a team, not to mention travel or work with
them."[32]

There were numerous other changes during Pincher Creek Colony's
early years. "I often wonder now-a-days how we got along without
electricity!"[33] The introduction of electricity to rural areas engendered
a profound change. Most indoor light had been provided by kerosene
lamps, whose wicks needed constant trimming, and whose globes
required perpetual cleaning. "Today this oil lamp is an expensive
antique and today's kids don't know what it is."[34]

The electrification of the region was not an overnight event. At first
only the town of Pincher Creek enjoyed full electrical service. The
power plant was coal-fired, with the large electrical turbines powered
by steam. "It was equipt [sic] with a steam whistle and at noon, twelve
o'clock by their time, right or wrong, they blew it."[35] It took years, but
eventually even very small communities received electrical service. By
virtue of their isolationist attitude toward the world, the Hutterian
bruderhofs were among the very last places to receive electricity.

> It took years to get the older generation to be persuaded
> by the younger generation to turn the gap, and install
> telephones and electricity. The first reproach was that it
> was from the devil, and the next was; that if we haven't
> gone broke so far, for sure we will get broke now.[36]

The influence of younger Hutterites on the colony has increased
steadily over the years. Though elders remain the primary decision-
makers, changes are most often suggested by those of the younger
generation. Paul Gross, now an elder, is perhaps more open to change

because he was an integral part of the movement for change by the younger generation at Pincher Creek.[37]

"So eventually the older folks got softer and agreed, . . ."[38] The decision in favor of electrification was reached on the condition that it would be used only in the places where it would be most beneficial: stock barns, to help give better care to the animals; chicken barns, so the hens could have "longer days," thus producing a greater quantity of eggs; and, of course, the school house.[39]

The Hutterites at Pincher Creek first electrified their bruderhof with a Jacobs Wind Power Generator. A set of batteries was used for back-up. For a time this was enough. "But time brings roses and changes."[40] As the colony electrified more of its buildings, more power was, of course, needed.

> From now on it wasen't [sic] too hard to persuade the elders to hook on to the main power line – but don't let the devil hook on appliances that don't please God.[41]

Electricity altered the face of the colony. It brought light to interiors that had previously been only dimly lit, and it brought warmth and comfort to chilly winter nights. It also led to the replacement of the "cooler," which had used ice. Before they adopted electricity, the Hutterites would hold "ice bees." They would invite their neighbors to the day-long event. A spot on the Castle River provided adequate ice, which was sawed into blocks measuring two feet by three feet by two feet. Horses would then haul the ice to the "cooler."

> Ice was stored and packed all around the cooler box, where all staples were kept on shelves, and covered and insulated with sawdust. This kept for an indefinite time till late fall or early winter. This was a common practice for years, till electric walk-in coolers and freezers were built.[42]

Electrification and mechanization also changed the mentality of the Hutterites. Other things, small and numerous, eventually found acceptance within their culture. The acceptance of changes by this bible-based society, however, was always arrived at by a democratic process. Paul Gross, in his book entitled *The Hutterite Way*, reflects on the impact of change within the broad scope of Hutterian history:

All the handy, worldly gadgets in the homes today would astonish our forefathers. If they could see us they would ask us whether we expected to come to the same heaven as they.[43]

## The Depression

The Great Depression ruined many people in rural areas, especially those who relied on a single livelihood. One of the worst situations was in the prairie region. Not only did the grain market collapse, but the environment followed soon after:

In 1931, the wind began lifting the topsoil in great black clouds. The next year brought the first great plague of grasshoppers, which devoured every green thing and clothing and tool handles besides. In 1933, drought, hail, rust, and frost joined the grasshoppers, as though all nature's forces had united in giving prairie settlers a notice to quit.[44]

Though closer to the mountains than to the prairies, the Pincher Creek Hutterites experienced the full impact of the Depression as well.[45]

Farmers planted their seed, but nothing became of it. There was no feed, and the Government had to send hay to many parts of the country to revive the stock cattle and horses for the winters were hard and many didn't make it.[46]

Government assistance, or "relief" as it was called, attempted to ease the burden. Relief camps and soup kitchens became an everyday sight. A few people were put to work, and a common daily wage was 25 cents. The price of food and other commodities fell, yet few people had enough money to purchase even necessities. "I remember we sold a cow with calf for $7.50, and the buyer, Earl Cook, was reluctant in buying more."[47] Paul recalls another irony during his Depression experience: "Strange to mention, coyote pelts sold for a good price; as high as $20.00 for a good pelt."[48] He took it upon himself to capitalize on this situation and became the trapper for the colony. "I had to tend my traps every day. This was one job that was not seasonal. I was a trapper for over fifty years."[49] This adaptive measure, along with the diversification of the Pincher Creek operation, enabled the Hutterites to weather the storm of the Great Depression.

The colony did not depend on grain alone for its existence. Departmental managers maintained successful operations raising steers for beef and hides; hogs for pork and bacon; sheep for mutton and wool; chickens and geese for poultry, eggs and down; and dairy cows for milk, butter, cream, and cheese. The two-acre garden produced virtually every type of vegetable that would grow in the Alberta climate. During the good years that were to come, the garden produced, "all kinds of vegetables, and there was a place in the bottom where you could irrigate. You could see it just about grow."[50]

The diligence with which the Hutterites at Pincher Creek worked assured their survival during the precarious Depression. Paul sums up the experience:

> In those trying years everybody had to pursue his own way of life in order to keep his head above the water of survival. A sharp pencil helped a lot. It was a time of "The Survival of the Fittest," and those that had saved, and knew how to save, survived.[51]

## Paul Gross – The Middle Years

"The Rocky Mountains are beautiful, the land is good, but there's a lot of wind."[52] With these words, Paul spoke of the region where he spent thirty-five years of his life. Paul was a strapping young lad of sixteen when he and his clan moved to Pincher Creek; here, he grew into manhood.

When his formal schooling ended, he was expected to work full time for the benefit of the community. He spent much of his youth trapping for furs. While this was not an agrarian pursuit, it helped to see the colony through hard times, and was such a lucrative enterprise that he continued to do it for many years. Once mechanization was accepted, Paul tended to his traplines in a jeep provided by the colony.[53]

Paul's first official vocation, mandated by an elder (most likely his father), was full charge of the chicken barn. He held responsibility for all facets of production and maintenance.[54] He was also assigned to the garden. Paul had great success maintaining the garden, employing many of the colony's children for assistance.

> I actually dearly loved to work with the kids. I had a pickup truck, and a little tractor with a trailer; the kids were always with me in the garden, when they weren't in school. It's surprising how much you can do with children.[55]

Hutterian life is largely governed by seasonal work. It is also thoroughly guided by their religion. At some point between eighteen years and the mid-twenties, at a time selected by the individual, Hutterites express the desire for baptism. They then embark on a rigorous course of instruction in religious doctrine and Hutterian history. Paul, following this tradition of his culture, received baptism on Sunday, March 24, 1929, at the age of 19.[56] He was now an adult, fully devoted to the Hutterite way.

For a Hutterite, baptism is the supreme rite of passage. With it, men become voting members of their community, and both men and women become marriageable. Moreover, baptism signifies a total voluntary adherence to the Hutterian creed which, presumably, remains in effect until death.

The other significant rite of passage is marriage. In the early bruderhofs of eastern Europe, couples were united in matrimony by the elders, without any previous introduction or element of courtship. The grounds for this practice were set forth in Peter Ridemann's *Confession of Faith*, written between 1540 and 1542:

> Concerning marriage . . . if this is to be done in a godly way they must come together not through their own action and choice, but in accordance with God's will and order, and therefore neither leave nor forsake the other but suffer both ill and good together all their days . . . Therefore . . . one should in no case choose from the flesh but await such a gift from God, and with diligence pray that God in accordance with his divine will might send what he from the beginning hath provided, serving to one's salvation and life. Then after such a prayer one should ask not his flesh but the elders that God might show him through them what he hath appointed for him.[57]

The custom of having one's marriage partner selected by the elders became less popular during the Thirty Years War (1618-1648), when the Hutterites' existence as a sect was at times in question. By the nineteenth century, in Russia, the custom ceased to exist.

Thus Paul, in the early 1930s, courted one Sarah Wollman.[58] Sarah, just one month shy of her twentieth birthday, was baptized on Sunday, April 9, 1933.[59] Paul, in keeping with the traditions of his culture, first asked his parents for permission to marry Sarah; then the minister was approached. Once consent was given all around, plans were discussed by the two families.[60] No formal wedding announcement was given until immediately prior to the ceremony. Paul and Sarah were wed on Sunday, August 13, 1933.[61] On that day Paul began to sign his name "Paul S. Gross," in observance of another Hutterian tradition: when a man marries, he uses the initial of his wife's first name in place of his middle name.[62]

As a practicing, baptized adult, Paul gained increased influence in his community. His interest in education became evident when he began attending the meetings of the school district's Board of Directors.

At the time of the colony's founding, the Hutterite children attended the school at Pincher Station. This was considered somewhat of an inconvenience. The time it took to pack lunches for the students, hitch the team to the wagon in which they all rode to and from the school, and the added attention to the needs of both children and animals, was an extra load on top of the daily work schedule at the colony. After a few years, a teacherage was built, and school was taught on the site by a qualified teacher licensed by the Department of Education.[63]

As teachers came and went and the school-age population grew, ". . . we asked to be admitted as an addition to the school district . . . [We] were turned down several times. Well, I harassed them plenty . . ."[64] Finally, a formal vote was put to the Board of Directors at a meeting attended by Paul. The vote, initiated by the school superintendent, who was sympathetic to the idea, was favorable and the move was made; ". . . all raised their hands, except the chairman, Ken McDowall, who was always the chief instigator against it."[65]

The name of the school was then discussed, and Paul told the board to name it The Sunset School.

> It was promised, that if there was no other such name in the Province of Alberta, it will be named thus. I thanked them for it; shook hands with all of them, but told Ken McDowall, that I had an ax to grind with him.[66]

Paul's involvement with educational matters was recognized by the elders: he was elected German school teacher by the voting membership of the colony.

> It was discussed for quite awhile as to who would be German school teacher. When they do this, they pick the best man they know; a man who is a writer, who knows grammar, especially German grammar – that's the hard thing. So finally the vote came around. I had all the votes.[67]

Paul attributes his election as German school teacher to the fact that he had high school training in South Dakota. "I passed the Lake Byron High School exams while studying for them at home."[68] In view of his scholastic ability, the colony had planned to send Paul to the college in Huron, South Dakota, the following year, 1924. That was, of course, the year in which the clan moved to Alberta; Paul never attended college, but the lack of a formal higher education did not impede his intellectual growth.

In Hutterian hierarchy, the German school teacher holds a highly visible position. It is an exalted occupation, commanding equal respect with that of the ministry. It is, in fact, a ministry in its own right, for the German school teacher inculcates the youth with their Hutterian identity through the teaching of Bible stories and Hutterian history in the German language.[69] The German teacher is also the disciplinarian of the colony. Discipline often necessitates the administration of corporal punishment: "We take heed of Solomon's injunction not to spare the rod lest we spoil the child."[70]

Though Paul, as disciplinarian, could punish his students, he also used shrewdness and tact to command obedience and respect from his charges. Paul reflected on his mentoring of the youth with these words:

> The greatest gift I have to give children is the knowl-edge that they can always look first to themselves for the answers to their problems. A child who develops an attitude which says, "I can probably find my own solutions, and if not, adults will be willing to give me some advice," becomes a survivor. This child usually has the edge in learning, relating to others, and making his/her way in the world.[71]

Paul's method of instilling confidence, a direct responsibility of the German school teacher, followed these steps:

1. Show understanding.
2. Ask, "How are you going to solve that problem?"
3. Share some choices.
4. Help him/her look at the consequences.
5. Give permission to solve it or not solve it.[72]

At any given time, Paul was in charge of an average of eighteen children. At times, when an English school teacher could not be found for the Pincher Creek Colony School, Paul did that job also.[73]

For a time, Paul's life was stable: he taught school, the colony grew and prospered, and, between 1934 and 1945, Sarah Gross gave birth to five children.[74]

Perhaps the greatest milestone in Paul Gross's life was his election to the ministry in 1949. When Paul became German teacher, he was elected to the position by the Pincher Creek Colony council. His nomination to the position of minister, however, was a more formal affair. Since the minister holds the highest position of authority in Hutterian culture, his election must be recognized by the entire leut.

> See, you call the bishop[75] and he gathers the elders together. A certain day is appointed and all the elders come to the colony to preside over the election. There are two candidates who are voted on. When the lot is cast, you have your answer. If one man has fewer than five votes, there's only one left. If they both have more than five votes, the lot is cast again.[76]

Paul's position as second minister was short lived, as he recalled:

> My uncle was the minister, but was kind of a sickly man. When I started in to preach, for one week, he died, and I was alone.[77]

It would be six years before Paul got an assistant. During these years he singlehandedly led his flock in their spiritual and temporal affairs. In addition to the obligations of the ministry, Paul also concentrated much of his time on writing.

> I wrote about sixty books, all in longhand German, all my sermons. Sometimes I wrote until three o'clock in the morning. My wife thought I was getting up. She'd say, "Are you getting up already?" I'd say, "Yes, I'm getting up." Then I'd get to bed.[78]

Paul's tirelessness as a writer exemplified the work ethic he took into all aspects of his ministry. Moreover, his election to this office was reflective of his total commitment to the Hutterite way.

## Maturity

Pincher Creek Colony matured with the passing of the years. The colony's land holdings increased through a combination of purchases, leases, and rentals, and its diverse operations enjoyed varying degrees of success. Throughout the lean years of the Depression, "everybody had the 'next year' disease; if it still failed this year, we will make it next year."[79]

The following years showed much more promise for the Hutterites: their crops grew, their animals thrived, and they renovated the colony's buildings.

> The homes were reconditioned inside and outside. A new hotel-style kitchen, containing the dining room for both adults and children, together with bakery was concrete-built.[80]

The kitchen was equipped with propane-burning appliances, even though, by the early 1940s, the entire colony received electricity from the East Kootenay Power Company's main line out of Fergie, British Columbia.[81] The completed kitchen complex included a full basement and an upstairs, "so all-told, a three-story structure."[82]

In 1940, a new hog barn was built, along with three chicken barns. The poultry production was so successful that the colony constructed an egg-grading station, ". . . as eggs could not be sold without knowing what's in them."[83] As the colony added more grain-producing land, they found it necessary to build several large granaries, which replaced the wooden ones erected in 1926. All these developments contributed to the success of the colony. Not all the changes were suggested by men: "Even milking machines were attached to the cows, for the women complained too, that they should have some labor-saving devising equiptment [sic]."[84]

Changes in Pincher Creek's membership occurred fairly early in its history. The original colony was comprised of ten Hofer families, two Wollman families, two Gross families and one Stahl family.[85]

> The Hofers had the advantage, and could outvote the other three [family groups], even though the others

merged. Since the Hutterite order is based on a democratic system and free enterprise, all matters of importance, such as electing officers, buying and selling and
other moves, is done by secret ballot. Therefore, the
Hofers won every round in the fight . . .[86]

As in any community, when the balance of power favors one particular
clan, discord and frustration emerge. For the Hutterian Brethren, the
solution to this is "branching out." Put in simplest terms, "branching
out" occurs when a portion of a colony, usually half, departs to
establish a new colony elsewhere.[87] Branching alleviates the problems
of burgeoning population growth, as well as those arising from fac-
tionalism, both of which were experienced at Pincher Creek. Consequently, only six years after helping to establish the Pincher Creek
bruderhof, ten of the Hofer families branched from the community and
moved eastward. Ironically, they moved right back to the Felger Farm
in Lethbridge. John Sandgren had put the farm up for sale, first giving
the Hutterites the option of buying it back:

> He approached us in the fall of 1932, that he would be
> willing to trade the Lucky Bell Ranch for the farm in
> Lethbridge, plus some over $100,000.00 difference. The
> former buildings were still there, ready for a colony to
> move in.[88]

An agreement was soon reached, and the Hofer families left Pincher
Creek, this time by truck.[89] This left the Pincher Creek community
somewhat understaffed. At the height of the Depression such a
situation was indeed precarious. This lack of manpower was met with
typical Hutterian tenacity, reflected in Paul Gross's words: "We were
now only a very few people. When time is pressed, you know, then
you take an extra load on you."[90]

Upon the departure of the Hofer families, new management was
immediately elected, including Jacob Wollman as managing director,
or "boss," and Paul Gross as German teacher. It was this administration
that led Pincher Creek Colony through the hard years of the Depression
and into the subsequent better years.

As the 1940s progressed, the population at Pincher Creek continued to increase; branching again became necessary to alleviate internal pressures. At the same time, World War II affected many nations, including Canada. The Hutterites once again claimed conscientious objection to war, but this time there was much less visible discrimination against them. There was, however, still a measure of fear and prejudice towards them. Citizens of Japanese descent were forcibly concentrated into special encampments, and those of German heritage experienced varying degrees of investigation. As North America suffered another wave of fear of "enemy aliens," and sought methods of maintaining wartime domestic security, the Hutterites again faced discrimination. This time persecution took the form of restrictive legislation directed toward their land purchases.[91]

The province of Alberta passed the Land Sales Prohibition Act in 1942. This measure was enacted to contain the growth of communities of "Hutterites and enemy aliens."[92] The act was introduced by Solon Low, an Alberta Mormon, who "argued that the legislation was designed to allay public feelings which had been aroused to the point of threatened violence."[93] It is, however, generally accepted that Low, at the urging of the Mormons in Alberta, acted out of fear of Hutterite colony expansions, as well as out of resentment toward the Hutterites' refusal to convert to Mormonism.[94] Actually, the Mormons possessed even greater tracts of land in the province than the Hutterites.[95] The Land Sales Prohibition Act was amended in 1943 to prohibit Hutterites from leasing land as well. Also in 1943, the act was ruled *ultra vires*, literally meaning "beyond strength," because the reference to "enemy aliens" was considered to be ambiguous.[96] In 1944, a new Land Sales Prohibition Act contained a specific reference to "Hutterites and Doukhobors."[97]

From the beginning, the Land Sales Prohibition Act was meant to be temporary legislation. "This bill is just a temporary expedient until an orderly arrangement can be worked out."[98] It was supposed to last until one year after the war. It actually remained in effect until 1947, when the Communal Property Act was adopted. The Land Sales Prohibition Act completely forbade the selling or leasing of land to Hutterites and Doukhobors, thus preventing their expansion. The Communal Property Act, on the other hand, put forth restrictions, including limiting the size of an individual colony to 6,400 acres, unless the colony had, before March 1, 1944, already owned more than that amount of land.[99] The act also prohibited the establishment of new colonies within forty miles of an existing colony, and it prohibited the establishment of any new Hutterian communities in the area south of Calgary where they were already concentrated.[100] Land acquisition by the Hutterites was made even more difficult by the Veterans Land Act of 1942, which provided for provincial assistance to veterans returning from the war who desired to enter into farming.[101] This act stated that land had to remain for sale on the open market for up to sixty days before it could be sold to the Hutterian Brethren.[102]

The direct result of this restrictive legislation was the pressing need for the Hutterites to seek land elsewhere. In 1952, numerous Hutterian communities from Alberta began to establish colonies in the neighboring province of Saskatchewan.[103] They immediately faced opposition similar to what they had left in Alberta. After several years of discussion, Pincher Creek Colony decided to look in a different direction:

> The years passed and the population in the colony got larger and were looking for land. Everybody complained about the forceful winds and hard winters in western Alberta . . . After scouting around the country and across the border, they chose the State of Washington for a site in Adams County, southwest of Ritzville.[104]

Though Paul wrote the above account in the third person, the move to Washington was undertaken primarily through his initiative.

# NOTES

1.    John Bennett, *Hutterite Brethren* (Stanford: Stanford University Press, 1967), 32.

2.    John Horsch, *The Hutterian Brethren, 1528-1931: A Story of Martyrdom and Loyalty* (Goshen, IN: Mennonite Historical Society, 1931), 115.

3.    David Flint, *The Hutterites: A Study in Prejudice* (Toronto: Oxford University Press, 1975), 83.

4.    Flint, *The Hutterites*, 83. The author of the act was Arthur Meighen, the Solicitor-General from Portage La Prairie, Manitoba. The quote is from his address to the House of Commons, September 6, 1917.

5.    Flint, *The Hutterites*, 84ff. For greater detail of the initial Hutterite experience in Canada, see Flint, Chapter 4, "Ethnic Conflict: 1914-20."

6.    John Hostetler, *Hutterite Society* (Baltimore: The Johns Hopkins University Press, 1974), 131.

7.    Paul Gross, interview with the author, November 15, 1991. Today, Spring Creek Hutterite Colony's 14,000 acre holdings spread out along the edge of the South Moccasin Mountains in the Judith Basin.

8.    Gross, interview with the author, November 15, 1991.

9.    Gross, interview with the author, November 15, 1991. Early in their American experience, some of the Schmiedeleut moved to Pennsylvania at the invitation of the Harmonists, another communal group which, by practicing celibacy, was diminishing in numbers. The experiment was not productive and the Hutterites moved back to South Dakota. In the late 1890s, with the advent of the Spanish American War, a group of Dariusleut established a short-lived colony in Manitoba; the threat of military conscription was present well before World War I.

10.   Gross, interview with the author, November 15, 1991.

11.   Gross, interview with the author, November 15, 1991.

12.   Gross, interview with the author, November 15, 1991.

13.   Paul Gross, *Pincher Creek Colony: Memories* (Pincher Creek: ALTA: By the author, n.d.), 4.

14.   Gross, *Memories*, 4.

15.   Gross, *Memories*, 5.

16. Gross, *Memories*, 5.

17. Gross, *Memories*, 6. Pete Hanson was involved in construction, which took up virtually all of his time. He had wanted to sell the farm for quite some time.

18. Gross, *Memories*, 6.

19. Gross, *Memories*, 9. It seems that the Hutterites made a fairly good choice. Many farmers in the area had to haul their entire water supply. Still, the Hutterian Brethren experienced periods of scant water.

20. Gross, *Memories*, 8. Specifically, Section 29, T6N, R30W.

21. Gross, *Memories*, 8.

22. Gross, *Memories*, 8.

23. The old building Paul speaks of had been at one time a barber shop and was moved to the ranch from Pincher Station in the late 1800s.

24. Gross, *Memories*, 9.

25. Gross, *Memories*, 11. For a diagram of a typical 20th century bruderhof, see Hostetler, *Hutterite Society*, 156, and Figure 2, page 73 in this volume.

26. Gross, *Memories*, 9.

27. Gross, *Memories*, 10.

28. The German-speaking Mennonites and the Doukhobors migrated from Russia to western North America at the same general time as did the Hutterites, for the same reasons. They were affected in the same way in Canada by the Wartime Elections Act of 1917. Perhaps their parallel experiences and common ethnicity explain their warm acceptance of one another.

29. Gross, *Memories*, 16. From this it can be inferred that the migration to Pincher Creek, besides the women and children who travelled by rail, was done entirely with horses.

30. Gross, *Memories*, 15.

31. Gross, *Memories*, 25.

32. Gross, *Memories*, 16.

33. Gross, *Memories*, 20.

34.    Gross, *Memories*, 20.

35.    Gross, *Memories*, 20.

36.    Gross, *Memories*, 21. Insulation from the world around them, coupled with a wary attitude toward change, is reflective of Hutterian, as well as Amish, practice throughout their histories. The old-order Amish still do not use electricity. Occasionally they will use a gas engine for some purposes, but only rarely and only if absolutely necessary. The Hutterites have accommodated many more twentieth century conveniences.

37.    The Dariusleut have found a middle-of-the-road attitude, generally speaking, between the more conservative Lehrerleut and the more liberal Schmiedeleut. My experience with Paul Gross's clan, in view of this, has been one of exposure to a relatively lenient group of Hutterian Brethren.

38.    Gross, *Memories*, 21.

39.    Gross, *Memories*, 21.

40.    Gross, *Memories*, 21.

41.    Gross, *Memories*, 21.

42.    Gross, *Memories*, 14.

43.    Paul Gross, *The Hutterian Way* (Saskatchewan: Freeman Publishing Company, Ltd., 1965), 73.

44.    Desmond Morton, *A Short History of Canada*, (Edmonton: Hurtig Publishers, Ltd., 1983), 179.

45.    Saskatchewan, the poorest province, suffered the most. Its farmland lost virtually all of its topsoil, which brought considerable actual starvation to its populace.

46.    Gross, *Memories*, 12.

47.    Gross, *Memories*, 13.

48.    Gross, *Memories*, 13.

49.    Paul Gross, interview with the author, November 23, 1991. Paul brought his vocation as trapper with him to Washington. In a letter to Leonard Gross, dated January 15, 1979, the letterhead of which reads, "Wolf-Coyote Trapping Instructor," Paul writes: "I am working on a very tight schedule in shipping Wolf-

Coyote-Fox bait and scent, together with trapping instructions and courses. Orders have never been that heavy. Fur prices are just beyond control. Bidders just go skyhigh (for) European and Japanese markets. At the same time I am still on the trapline. Next year is my 50th anniversary in trapping instructing and lure manufacturing . . ." In a response dated May 8, 1979, Leonard Gross reflects on Hutterian adaptation to their environment: ". . . the Hutterites continue to amaze me, regarding the variety of vocations and the creative approach to life that simply surfaces from time to time." (Leonard Gross MSS. Archives of the Mennonite Church, Goshen, IN. Executive Secretary Correspondence. Box 6, Folder 43: Paul Gross, 1971 - _____.).

50. Paul Gross, interview with the author, November 15, 1991. Paul was the "garden man" for a time, as will be evident later in the chapter.

51. Gross, *Memories*, 17.

52. Paul Gross, interview with the author, November 15, 1991.

53. Paul Gross, interview with the author, November 23, 1991.

54. Paul Gross, interview with the author, November 15, 1991.

55. Paul Gross, interview with the author, November 15, 1991.

56. *Dariusleut Colony Genealogies*: Colony #46 – Espanola, 1.

57. Peter Ridemann, *Confessions of Faith* (London: Hodder & Stoughton; Rifton, NY: Plough Publishing House, 1950), 97-98, 100.

58. Sarah Wollman was born at Huron Colony, Huron, South Dakota, on May 9, 1913.

59. *Dariusleut Colony Genealogies*: Colony #46 – Espanola, 1.

60. For detailed discussion of twentieth century Hutterian marriage practices, see Hostetler, *Hutterite Society*, 237-240.

61. *Dariusleut Colony Genealogies*: Colony #46 – Espanola, 1. Formal religious ceremonies take place at the Sunday service, though a religious service is held every day.

62. William Gross, interview with the author, October 25, 1991. Not all Hutterite men adopt this practice; it is largely a matter of individual choice.

63. Gross, *Memories*, 18. A teacherage was a house built specifically for an outside teacher to live in on the colony grounds.

64. Gross, *Memories*, 34.

65. Gross, *Memories*, 34.

66. Gross, *Memories*, 34-35.

67. Paul Gross, interview with the author, November 15, 1991.

68. Paul Gross, interview with the author, November 15, 1991.

69. The need for both German and English school teachers is a North American phenomenon reached through educational legislation and the powerful dynamics of assimilation, which dictate the obligation to conduct one's life in the English language. The Hutterites have met this challenge most effectively, by adhering to the laws while also conducting German school.

70. Paul Gross, *The Hutterite Way*, 71.

71. Paul Gross, interview with the author, April 4, 1992.

72. Paul Gross, interview with the author, April 4, 1992.

73. Paul Gross, interview with the author, November 15, 1991.

74. Sarah, born Thursday, May 24, 1934.
Barbara, born Tuesday, July 7, 1936.
Maria, born Friday, March 17, 1939.
William, born Monday, April 22, 1940.
Frank, born Saturday, October 20, 1945.
*Dariusleut Colony Genealogies*: Colony #46 – Espanola, 1. Five children is well below the Hutterian family average of ten children. Jacob and Elizabeth Gross, Paul's brother and sister-in-law, had thirteen children between 1937 and 1961. *Dariusleut Colony Genealogies*: Colony #46 – Espanola, 5.

75. The Bishop of the Dariusleut is John Wurz, who resides at the Wilson Side Colony in Lethbridge, Alberta. Today, he is one of the very few Dariusleut people who surpass Paul Gross in age.

76.  Paul Gross, interview with the author, November 23, 1991.

77.  Paul Gross, interview with the author, November 23, 1991.

78.  Paul Gross, interview with the author, November 23, 1991. Paul, in keeping with Hutterian tradition, borrowed sermon books from other ministers in order to hand copy their texts. The job is a formidable one and often lasts the rest of a minister's life. Paul now has close to 300 sermons in his personal collection.

79.  Gross, *Memories*, 33.

80.  Gross, *Memories*, 33.

81.  Gross, *Memories*, 33.

82.  Gross, *Memories*, 33.

83.  Gross, *Memories*, 33. Up until then, eggs were graded by candlelight.

84.  Gross, *Memories*, 33. The dairy operation was formerly a manual affair: "The milking and separating of milk was done by hand. There were as many as 20 to 25 milk cows, more or less, and each woman had 4 cows to milk, morning and evening. There was a double shift each week." 13.

85.  Gross, *Memories*, 11.

86.  Gross, *Memories*, 11. It should be reemphasized that only adult baptized men vote in the Hutterite culture.

87.  Branching is not a simple occurrence. For detailed descriptions, see Kephart, *Extraordinary Groups*, 272-275, and Hostetler, *Hutterite Society*, 185-190.

88.  Paul Gross, *Memories*, 30. The Hutterites at Pincher Creek changed the name of the Laughlin Bell Ranch to the Lucky Bell Ranch soon after they took over.

89.  Gross, *Memories*, 11.

90.  Paul Gross, interview with the author, November 15, 1991.

91.  Hostetler, *Hutterite Society*, 133.

92.  Select Committee of the Assembly (Communal Property), *Report on Communal Property* (Edmonton, ALTA: 1927), 6. Hereinafter cited as *R.C.P.*

93.   Hostetler, *Hutterite Society*, 133.

94.   Paul Gross, interview with the author, January 29, 1992. "On the other hand, some highly placed Mormons, including men in the Alberta government, opposed the legislation and later sought its revision." Bennett, *Hutterian Brethren*, 32-33.

95.   Hostetler, *Hutterite Society*, 133.

96.   *R.C.P.*, 6.

97.   *R.C.P.*, 6. The new act was considered *intra vires*, literally meaning "within strength," thus justifiable.

98.   Quote of Solon Low in *Edmonton Journal*, 17 March 1942, in Flint, *The Hutterites*, 123.

99.   *R.C.P.*, 7.

100.  *R.C.P.*, 7.

101.  Flint, *The Hutterites*, 111.

102.  *R.C.P.*, 7.

103.  *R.C.P.*, 11.

104.  Paul Gross, *Memories*, 35.

## Chapter 5

# WASHINGTON –
# THE PROMISED LAND

When the Hutterian Brethren contemplate branching, the process begins with many discussions among the menfolk.

> This process requires delicate management of capital assets and investments, redistribution of colony authority, and careful attention to kinship factors and work patterns.[1]

The branching of the Pincher Creek bruderhof was precipitated by the size of the colony's population, which had grown to maximum capacity by the mid-1950s. The Communal Property Act, which forced them to look beyond the borders of Alberta, had a dramatic effect on the branching process.

During the early, investigative period of branching, some members of the colony went to Chihuahua, Mexico, to look at land supposedly owned by some real estate agents in Vancouver, British Columbia.[2] The Hutterite delegation spent several weeks in January and February of 1950 looking at land. No land was purchased as the result of this journey because, as it turned out, the real estate agents were dishonest: ". . . they didn't speak the truth; the land that they had for sale wasn't their land."[3] The Hutterian Brethren had made the mistake of giving a down payment of approximately $60,000 to the real estate agents before actually seeing any farmland.

> So when our people found out that they were beat – that they were cheated through a crooked deal – they reported it to the government in Chihuahua which went

after those land agents from Mexico City and from Vancouver. Each colony had paid $10,000 down and only got $3,000 back. The rest we lost.[4]

The Hutterites, in their desperate need for expansion, looked for land in many places. Paul's brother-in-law, Elias Wollman, suggested that they investigate Saskatchewan, as many of the other colonies were doing. Paul was not agreeable to a move to Saskatchewan: "If you want to go to Saskatchewan, you go. I'm not going. There's about fifty colonies in Saskatchewan already."[5] A delegation from Pincher Creek did go to Saskatchewan to look at land, but they did so without Paul. "They found some land there, but I didn't allow for a move there."[6] Then the State of Montana was suggested, to which Paul responded:

> I was raised in Montana and I don't want to go to Montana. It's the biggest mountain country – a lot of scabrock. If you want Montana you go. I'll not be going with you.[7]

The idea of anyone going anywhere without Paul was laughable. His advice was to ". . . just stay quiet. There are quite a few ranches for sale in the world."[8]

Eventually an unforeseen catalyst directed the group's attention to the State of Washington. Another crooked businessman, this time a grain broker, entered the picture.

> He must have sold over half a million dollars worth of hybrid wheat to our people in Alberta – dryland grain that yielded a good harvest, you know – and everybody bought it, everybody. Well, he couldn't deliver, so we looked for him and found him in Washington.[9]

Telephone contact was made, and the man disclosed that he had neither the grain nor the money. The Hutterites immediately went to their attorney, who contacted a lawyer in Tacoma. When it was discovered that the agent had a home in Sunnyside, in the Yakima Valley, the lawyers decided to put a $5,000 lien on it. At that point, the man decided to negotiate with the Hutterites. "You come down to Sunnyside and we'll talk."[10]

Paul Gross and Eli Wollman travelled to the Yakima Valley by bus. They conferred with the man, who agreed to return the money he owed them if they would release the lien on his house.

During this visit, the man, who owned a twin-engine airplane, offered to show them land throughout south-central Washington.

> Well we got into his plane and we looked at land, but you don't see much from the air. We did see lots of land – grass covered hills – but it didn't suit us. So we went home and decided to return with a car.[11]

At some point during the search for a new home, Paul Gross set his sights firmly on the State of Washington. As Paul recalled, the aerial view of the land helped him decide: "In the back of my mind I had it; since we couldn't buy land in Alberta where we wanted, this could be our future home."[12] Also, Washington had been a familiar name to him since his childhood.

> In the late 1800s when the railroad was being built out here, my great-uncle left his home in South Dakota and came west. During that time, the railroad was constructed in the daytime, and the Indians would tear it up at nighttime – so the going was slow. Well, the end of the line for my great-uncle was right here in Washington. He loved it so much that he didn't want to go back to Dakota; they had to come get him.[13]

Paul always remembered his great-uncle's stories about Washington. "He told me Washington was a paradise. Good land, good water, good climate. When we were looking for those things, I remembered what he had said.[14]

The Pincher Creek Hutterites made three trips to Washington to look for farmland. The last journey proved fruitful, though it did not seem so at first. They were actually on their way back to Canada when they stopped for a night's rest in Ritzville.

> . . . we couldn't find anything that was suitable. I stayed up in the hotel lobby and read a paper – almost went to sleep. A man came up to me and said, "Do you know the Mennonites?" I replied, "We're cousins to the

Mennonites. We're Hutterians. We're staying overnight
and we're looking for land."[15]

The man with whom Paul spoke said that he knew of a ranch for sale.
It was located fifteen miles west of Ritzville; the man who operated the
ranch wanted to either sell or rent the place because his hips were
giving out. Paul asked for a description of the man and his land, and
a map with which to find the place. The man told him:

> "You go into this area and ask for Clarence Hagen.
> Anyone you speak with will tell you where he lives."
> So the next day the boys got up and were ready to go
> home. There was four inches of snow on the ground.
> "No," I said. "We're not going home. I found a ranch
> and we're going to look at it today."[16]

They drove west into "Mennonite territory,"[17] and located the home of
Clarence Hagen.

> We had on big coats, you know; it was cold. Big coats,
> caps, and beards. He was in his orchard pruning his
> trees. I said, "Mr. Hagen? Hagen Ranch? Clarence
> Hagen?" He looked at us and said, "Are you from
> Mars? What do you want?" I said to him, "We stayed
> overnight in Ritzville and a land agent by the name of
> Smith said your ranch was for sale or rent." Hagen said
> to us, "I'll sell or rent to you, either way you want." Six
> of us went into the house. He had two kids there; they
> were afraid of us, you know.[18]

Both the Hutterites and Clarence Hagen were interested in proceeding
with negotiations, but the Hutterites took a cautious approach.

> The owner was ready to negotiate but we were not
> ready for we had to have more information as to his
> legal ownership. He was ready to see his lawyer, but we
> were not legally prepared to deal with him.[19]

Also, Paul Gross had to defend the choice of land to his brethren.
Migration to Washington was considered an almost rebellious move by
other Hutterites in Alberta. It involved actually crossing the Rocky
Mountains, something that had never been done before. Most of the

Dariusleut men voiced their opinion in favor of moving to Saskatchewan or Montana. The majority thought that Washington was out of the question. Usually, by Hutterian tradition, the majority would have the absolute support of the bishop. In this instance, such was not the case.

> For this transaction, the matter had to be brought before
> our bishop and elders in Alberta. However, the bishop
> was a good friend of mine and it wasn't hard to per-
> suade him, but his assistant elders were hard to per-
> suade. They said: "Paul Gross will become a renegade.
> For the sheep that strays from the flock, becomes a prey
> to the wolves."[20]

Paul maintained his independence of mind, and successfully defended his position, noting that a congestion of Hutterian colonies in any single location was neither "healthy nor wealthy."[21] Moreover, Washington did not have restrictive legislation directed towards the Hutterites, as did Alberta. He further noted that Saskatchewan and South Dakota were attempting to ratify legislation similar to Alberta's. In Paul's opinion, "it . . . would be detrimental to move to such areas."[22]

In the end, he was given approval for the move, and negotiations for land purchases and leases in Washington proceeded, using attorneys representing each party. As the Hutterites were planning to relocate permanently in Washington, they needed a lawyer in that area, one who could successfully represent them and advocate on their behalf. With the assistance of Clarence Hagen, they located a lawyer in Ritzville named Leonard F. Jansen.[23] He recalled his first introduction to the Hutterites:

> One day in the summer of 1955, I was in my office in
> Ritzville, when suddenly the door opened and in walked
> about ten or twelve bearded men with black hats and
> black suits accompanied by Clarence Hagen. I said to
> myself, "My God! What hath God wrought?" Come to
> find out, they were the Hutterian Brethren of Pincher
> Creek, Alberta, Canada. Clarence said to me, "I'm going
> to lease the John L. Fox farm to these people and
> you've got to become their lawyer."[24]

Jansen agreed, beginning a business relationship which would last more than thirty-five years.

In the Spring of 1956, the land was transferred. Clarence Hagen "was willing to sell part of his estate and give the rest to us on a long-term lease with option to buy."[25] The arrangement consisted of a purchase from Hagen of:

> . . . about 800 acres of land, some of it irrigable, including 320 acres west of Schrag and 480 acres south of Highway 10 on the Adams-Grant County line. In addition, they have leased 3800 acres owned by Mrs. Hagen, including the Hagen home farm north of Lind. The five-year lease is on a share-crop basis, Mrs. Hagen said.[26]

In Washington the Hutterites had to deviate from their tradition of dry-land farming. The land they purchased was all irrigation land, but they had never before irrigated their farmlands. With typical efficiency, they learned to farm irrigated land.

> The farmer will have to be adaptable to crops and methods that can get the price and not what he wants to grow or thinks he can only grow . . . We learned to use it the hard way, but it's important to have good timing and efficiency with an irrigation system and I think the communal colony can handle that very well.[28]

Most of the Hutterites' land acquisition, however, was leased, and was suitable for dry-land agriculture. They launched into their wheat growing operation and, by early August, "were bringing in their first grain harvest."[29] That autumn, they also enjoyed the bounty of their vegetable and fruit harvests.[30]

The Hutterites' enterprise in Washington was experimental. As such, only two families were involved in the initial move. Elias Wollman was the patriarch of the group.

> The eight members of his family and the five in the family of his son, Jacob, are its nucleus. Two nephews, Mike and Sammy Gross, and two girls from the parent colony in Pincher Creek are with them to help get the

community organized and aid with the wheat harvest. All 17 live in the former Hagen home and an adjacent bunkhouse.[31]

In contrast to their earlier sojourn in the United States, this time the Hutterites did not experience animosity from the local people.

> People from the Methodist, Mennonite and Lutheran churches came to visit us. They were very kind. There has been no objection against us whatever.[32]

The warm welcome they received in their new home was comforting, but the Hutterites knew from experience that their survival was not dependent on the friendliness of their neighbors. The conviction that Washington was indeed a good choice for their relocation was affirmed by the success of their agriculture.

> Here, it's a longer and better season, a milder winter. We can grow much more than we could at home. That's the advantage we have.[33]

Though the move from Canada was relatively smooth, it was not without opposition. After the migration to Canada in the wake of the First World War, Hutterites did not settle again the United States in any substantial numbers until after the Second World War. In the intervening years, the United States government had made provisions for conscientious objectors,[34] but the Immigration and Naturalization Service, showing characteristically American xenophobia, stubbornly fought the repatriation of the Hutterites. They had, however, a competent legal mediator in Leonard Jansen, who successfully engineered their immigration.

> I'm the reason that they are here now; I enabled them to return to the United States because they were either born in the United States or were born of American parents. We had many a battle with the immigration service over this . . .[35]

Jansen's legal advocacy made it easier for more Hutterites to immigrate to Washington; the next group, however, did not come for five years.

During those five years, the experiment in Washington "proved to be a success."[36] The farming operation they conducted was enormous; "to operate the huge tract we needed all the help we could procure from the home colony."[37] Seasonal work parties came and went, and eventually the Pincher Creek Hutterites decided to make plans for a fully-established bruderhof.

Paul Gross, although he was their minister, did not initially move to Washington with the Wollman families:

> I travelled back and forth, several times a month. Then, after a few years, the elders said, 'It's no good – only two families there. You'd better do something about it.' So I had to move.[38]

Between 1956 and 1959 the group continued to look for a large dry-land farm to buy.[39] Being committed to living in Washington, the Hutterites searched throughout the Big Bend country, as well as farther east and in the Palouse region. Meanwhile they continued their farming operation near Lind, buying and selling machinery in their effort to keep abreast of the latest technology. A farm machinery salesman told the Hutterites of a place for sale near the Deep Creek community west of Spokane. It belonged to Alvin P. Brende, owner of the Brende Machinery Company of Spokane.[40] Brende began selling tracts of land to Hutterites in May, 1960. Within a month, they had bought six tracts of land and had leased several others, totaling approximately 3,000 acres (see Figures 3, 4, and 5, pages 74, 75, and 76).[41]

In January of 1960, the Hutterites' Board of Trustees had filed their Articles of Incorporation. These articles, signed by Paul Gross, Jacob Wollman, and Elias Wollman, and notarized by their attorney, Leonard Jansen, organized the Hutterian Brethren of Spokane as a full religious corporation under sanction of Chapter 24.08 of the Revised Code of Washington (see Appendix F, page 117). By legally incorporating themselves, the Hutterites were recognized as

> . . . a body politic and corporate, with perpetual succession, they shall be capable, in law, of suing and being sued, pleading and being impleaded, answering and being answered in all the courts of the state; they

may have a common seal, alter and change the same at pleasure; acquire, mortgage and sell property, personal and real, for the purpose of carrying out the objects of the corporation, and make bylaws, rules and regulations, as they may deem proper and best for the welfare and the good order of the corporation; and may amend the articles of incorporation by supplemental articles, executed and filed the same as the original articles: *Provided*, That such bylaws, rules and regulations be not contrary to the Constitution and laws of the United States, and the existing laws of the state.[42]

So it was as a corporation, with all the benefits that implies, that the Hutterites purchased the land in Spokane County. They began plans for the construction of the new bruderhof's buildings, obtaining the necessary building permits from the county in the summer. Work on the property did not begin for six months, not until the late autumn of 1960.[43] From November of 1960 through January of 1961, the Wollman families moved to the new site from the farm near Lind, and the Pincher Creek Colony formally branched, with approximately half of the families moving to the Deep Creek property.[44] "At Pincher Creek [a] new manager was elected together with his board, as the management had choosen [sic] to move to Washington."[45]

There were now sixty Hutterites permanently residing in Washington.[46] During the construction of the buildings, the members of the community lived in temporary quarters, but before long they moved into their completed living units. At the time of Pincher Creek's founding in 1926, Hutterite work parties came from throughout Alberta to help construct new buildings. At Deep Creek, also called Espanola Colony, a new approach to the construction was adopted.

Sometime in 1959, Elias Wollman had noticed a prefabricated building on one of his visits to Spokane. This building was for sale and Wollman wanted to buy it and have it moved to the Hutterite farm in Lind. Inquiries led to the introduction of the Hutterites to Bestway Building Supply in Spokane, a subsidiary of Boise Cascade.[47] After the building permits for Deep Creek Colony were secured, and the families had moved to the site, the Hutterites contracted Bestway to build prefabricated structures for them, at their plant in Spokane. These were then moved to the colony for assembly and erection.[48] The Hutterites were, of course, involved with the project as well:

> All these buildings, and the homes too, were built in Spokane – the whole place, built in Spokane. We laid the foundations and Bestway Building Center brought the buildings here and set them up. Their pencils were sharper than ours . . .[49]

The contractor in charge of the operation was a young man, recently graduated from Washington State College, named Stan Sloan.

> I helped build that colony; I was, for the most part, the main contractor for that whole project. Eli Wollman said to my boss: "I have never put as much trust in anyone as I have in that young man." When he said this, he was pointing to me.[50]

Sloan, his work crew, and the Hutterite men assembled three duplexes, "each suitable for two or three families."[51] Several additional buildings were erected by the summer of 1961. These included a dining hall, which contained a kitchen, a bakery, a large walk-in freezer, and two dining rooms; a chicken house; a barn; a poultry processing plant; a machine shop; a school house; a laundry; and a dairy barn.[52] Hutterian orderliness was expressed in the orientation of all the buildings perpendicular to a north-south line (see Figure 2, page 73).

The estimated value of the buildings, as listed on the permits, was over $72,000.[53] This was a considerable sum of money then, even more than it is now. Stan Sloan, however, estimated the actual cost of construction substantially higher.

> I can tell you right now that $72,000 doesn't come close to the actual price tag for that colony. More than once, Eli Wollman placed $10,000, in cash, into my hands, to come into Spokane to buy equipment or supplies for the colony. After the place was as complete as it was going to be for a while, I'd have to say that the Hutterites spent over $300,000 on their community.[54]

# Figure 2

## Diagram of Deep Creek Colony

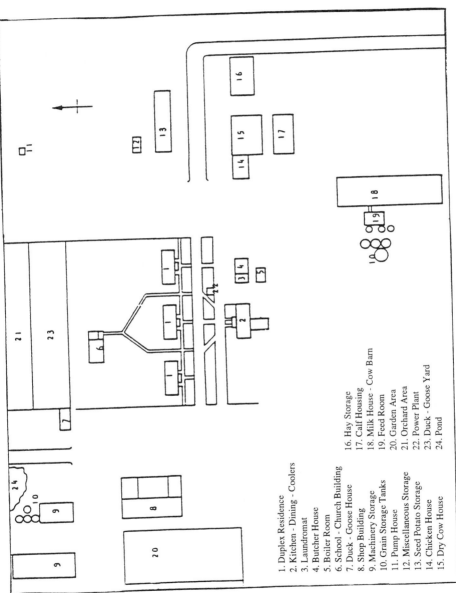

1. Duplex Residence
2. Kitchen - Dining - Coolers
3. Laundromat
4. Butcher House
5. Boiler Room
6. School - Church Building
7. Duck - Goose House
8. Shop Building
9. Machinery Storage
10. Grain Storage Tanks
11. Pump House
12. Miscellaneous Storage
13. Seed Potato Storage
14. Chicken House
15. Dry Cow House
16. Hay Storage
17. Calf Housing
18. Milk House - Cow Barn
19. Feed Room
20. Garden Area
21. Orchard Area
22. Power Plant
23. Duck - Goose Yard
24. Pond

## Figure 3

### Portion of Deep Creek Quadrangle Showing Colony Location
from U.S. Geological Survey map

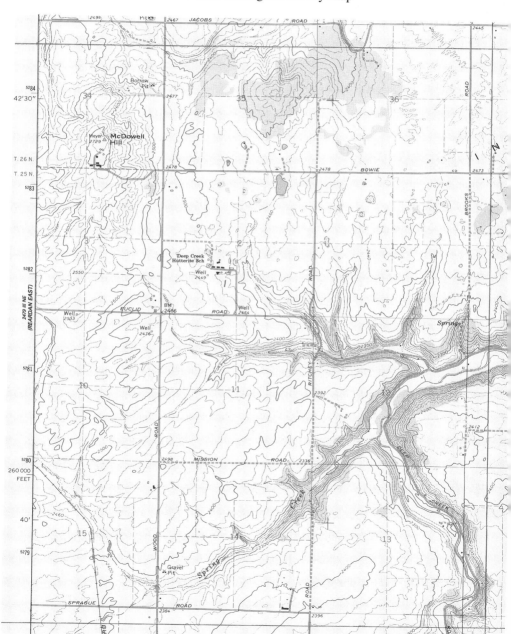

## Figure 4
### Initial Land Purchases of 1960
### by the Hutterian Brethren of Spokane (HBS), Inc.

| DATE | GRANTOR | SEC. TWP. RG. | DEED NO. |
|------|---------|---------------|----------|
| 5-31-60 | Brende Mac. Co. | 34-T26N-R40E | 768-388 |
| 6-3-60 | Brende Mac. Co. | 4-T25N-R40E | 768-552 |
| 6-9-60 | Alvin P. Brende | 10-T25N-R40E | 768-727 |
| 6-10-60 | Brende Mac. Co. | 4-T25N-R40E | 768-769 |
| 6-13-60 | Alvin P. Brende | 15-T25N-R40E | 769-47 |
| 7-1-60 | Alvin P. Brende | 2-T25N-R40E | 769-672 |

(Spokane County Auditor, General Index-Direct-Spokane County, Washington. Grantee H-K, 1960-1967, Folio 61)

# Figure 5

## Statutory Warranty Deed:
## First Purchase by the Hutterian Brethren of Spokane, Inc.

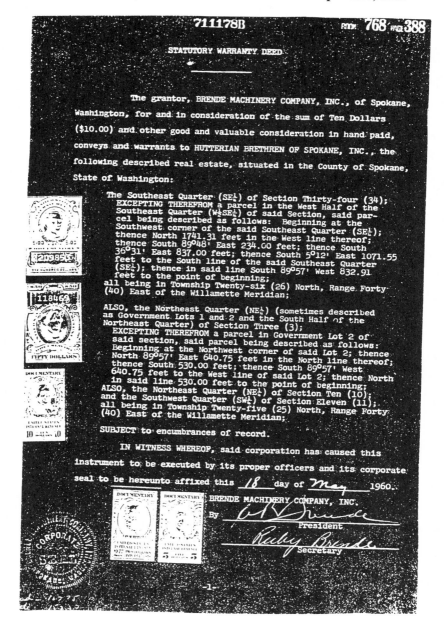

711178B                                                   РПЮК 768 ᴘᴀɢᴇ 388

### STATUTORY WARRANTY DEED

The grantor, BRENDE MACHINERY COMPANY, INC., of Spokane, Washington, for and in consideration of the sum of Ten Dollars ($10.00) and other good and valuable consideration in hand paid, conveys and warrants to HUTTERIAN BRETHREN OF SPOKANE, INC., the following described real estate, situated in the County of Spokane, State of Washington:

The Southeast Quarter (SE¼) of Section Thirty-four (34); EXCEPTING THEREFROM a parcel in the West Half of the Southeast Quarter (W½SE¼) of said Section, said parcel being described as follows: Beginning at the Southwest corner of the said Southeast Quarter (SE¼); thence North 1741.31 feet in the West line thereof; thence South 89°48' East 234.00 feet; thence South 36°31' East 837.00 feet; thence South 5°12' East 1071.55 feet to the South line of the said Southeast Quarter (SE¼); thence in said line South 89°57' West 832.91 feet to the point of beginning; all being in Township Twenty-six (26) North, Range Forty (40) East of the Willamette Meridian;

ALSO, the Northeast Quarter (NE¼) (sometimes described as Government Lots 1 and 2 and the South Half of the Northeast Quarter) of Section Three (3); EXCEPTING THEREFROM a parcel in Government Lot 2 of said section, said parcel being described as follows: Beginning at the Northwest corner of said Lot 2; thence North 89°57' East 640.75 feet in the North line thereof; thence South 530.00 feet; thence South 89°57' West 640.75 feet to the West line of said Lot 2; thence North in said line 530.00 feet to the point of beginning; ALSO, the Northeast Quarter (NE¼) of Section Ten (10); and the Southwest Quarter (SW¼) of Section Eleven (11); all being in Township Twenty-five (25) North, Range Forty (40) East of the Willamette Meridian;

SUBJECT to encumbrances of record.

IN WITNESS WHEREOF, said corporation has caused this instrument to be executed by its proper officers and its corporate seal to be hereunto affixed this _18_ day of _May_ 1960.

BRENDE MACHINERY COMPANY, INC.

By _____
                              President

_____
                              Secretary

-1-

Once the buildings were finished, the Brethren settled down to their communal, pacifistic way of life, ironically, living right next to the Air Force missile sites of the Spokane Air Defense Sector. This did not bother them; they knew the adjacent land had been set aside for military purposes when they bought their place. Paul Gross echoed a typical Hutterian attitude when he said, "We are not concerned about things of the world . . ."[55]

While the Hutterites had received a cordial welcome when they first arrived in Washington, they now faced trouble with their neighbors. The problem was attributable once again to fear and misunderstanding of strangers by mainstream Americans, in this case the agricultural community surrounding the Hutterite colony near Spokane. The *Spokesman-Review* published an article which focused considerable negative attention on the Hutterites.

> All is not well in the rolling Espanola country west of Spokane where the strangely somber Hutterite people formed a new American colony two years ago. The older families in the picturesque farm country have been growing uneasy of late over the presence in their midst of a "different people" whose religion, customs and mode of dress are strangely removed from the American viewpoint.[56]

This antagonism had first been expressed by the local farmers when the Hutterites began buying land from Alvin Brende. Leonard Jansen recalls the early stages of the confrontation:

> They [the Hutterites] were able to pay fifty dollars more per acre than what the land was selling for. This advantage gave them considerable leverage over local farmers who may have wanted to negotiate with Brende for his land. They were, in the view of the people of the vicinity, "foreigners," "different," "not to be trusted." This misunderstanding in some people often led to hatred.[57]

The *Spokesman-Review* told the same story:

> . . . it is the outcropping of deep feelings of resentment
> on the part of Espanola farm families against what they
> consider an invasion by strangers.[58]

The farming community chose to combat this "encroachment" by proposing to limit Hutterian expansion through the familiar method of restrictive legislation.

> About 200 members of Spokane County Grange #4,
> meeting at Greenbluff Grange Hall, went on record
> unanimously in favor of a communal property law in the
> State of Washington.[59]

This law, if enacted, would have restricted property ownership by communal groups. The members of the Grange intended to present a formal petition at their statewide meeting in Bellingham, with the hope of introducing the measure to the state legislature. At the same time, locals who opposed the Hutterites printed derogatory literature and began to spread rumors about them.[60]

Throughout the Hutterites' history, land has been of paramount importance. After the Dariusleut settled in Washington, they tried to acquire more and more land for their large-scale farming operation. In view of this, the proposed measure by the members of the Grange, though not unfamiliar to the Hutterites, was potentially quite restrictive.

> The purpose of the Grange petition is to put an end to
> the Hutterite practice of communal farms on which the
> land, crops and equipment are owned – not by an in-
> dividual – but "for the common use."[61]

Paul Gross questioned the alleged threat of Hutterite expansion:

> Does this seem outlandish? I know of many farm
> families who own much more. We are all American
> citizens . . . It would seem that we have the right to
> farm as much land as we can acquire.[62]

The surrounding community was determined to keep the Hutterites from gaining additional lands. Misconceptions about the Hutterian Brethren often originate with people who live close to them;[63] during this incident the most vocal antagonist was Mrs. Ethel Peterson, "whose farm on Jacobs Road abuts the Hutterite property."[64] Mrs. Peterson's concerns were a central feature of the newspaper article. In it, she is quoted describing the Hutterites as:

> ". . . the world's oldest Communists," and followers of a system wherein all property is vested in the community and all labor practiced for the common good.[65]

Two specific elements of Hutterian practice, corporate purchasing power, and low-cost labor from their members, enabled them to buy good land at high prices. This led to resentment by the local farmers who did not have their buying power. There were additional allegations:

> They claim religion as their basis . . . They have registered in the state as a church but have no affiliations or missions with any churches or sects other than their own . . . Our main objection is that they operate a farm under the guise of religion . . . They want and get many concessions taxwise that permit them to make more money. Then they turn around and try to pressure us into selling them our farms.[66]

It is true that the Hutterian Brethren were active in their land search, and they were definitely wealthy in the corporate sense, but they did not put pressure on farmers to sell their lands. Moreover, allegations of religion being a guise were unfounded.[67]

Considering the American hysteria about Communism at the time, describing the Hutterian Brethren as "the world's oldest Communists" was a powerful denunciation. Mrs. Peterson defended her accusation:

> Mrs. Peterson, pointing to the Russian background of the ancient religious sect, calls attention to the fact that the Hutterite land virtually surrounds two Air Force missile sites which are vital components of the Spokane Air Defense Sector. "You wonder if they bought their land close to missile sites by accident or by design."[68]

As spokeswoman for the farmers against the Hutterian Brethren of Spokane, Ethel Peterson was effective at gaining support in opposing them. All the same, the Hutterites remained characteristically calm in the face of the social opposition they encountered. Paul Gross, as spiritual leader and spokesman for the group, referring to the measure proposed by the Grange, told the *Spokesman-Review*:

> We will do nothing to fight them . . . We do not care to become involved in matters such as this. We believe in the old saying, "live and let live." We will let this matter take its own course, and in the meantime, we will go about our business as usual.[69]

Leonard Jansen, however, was not content to let the issue rest.

> This is outright religious persecution . . . of a group of fine people who want nothing more than to do their work and mind their own business. Somebody is going to get sued . . . unless all of this persecution is stopped immediately.[70]

When the *Spokesman-Review* published its article on May 27, 1962, the Hutterites and their attorney, considering it a defamation of character, sued the newspaper.

> We brought suit against the paper for publishing incorrect statements, chief of which was their [the Hutterites] being called Communists. We won the modest sum of $3,000 as well as a public retraction and apology by the *Spokesman-Review*. I was never so pleased in my life as I was to see Bill Cowles and his editorial staff quake at the prospect of being sued.[71]

The retraction by the newspaper did not stop the litigation between the Hutterian Brethren of Spokane and the *Spokesman-Review*, but it was a formal, public apology.

> The *Spokesman-Review* holds no belief that the members of the Hutterite colony are anything other than substantial, responsible and loyal citizens of the United States. If the article reported viewpoints tending to impugn the reputation of the members of the colony, it was not the intention of the newspaper to do so, and it expresses regret and apologizes in that circumstance.[72]

The proposal for restrictive legislation never materialized. The Hutterian Brethren of Spokane were vindicated, and Paul Gross admonished his brethren to "never do anything without your lawyer."[73] After this episode, life on the Hutterite farm settled back into its regular schedule of hard work and prayer.

During the early years in Washington, the Hutterites learned newer, more effective methods of farming, "which included such practices as fertilizing, seed treatment, and different methods of planting and tilling the soil."[74] Combined with their experiment in irrigation on the farm in Lind, their farming activities were time consuming indeed. They retained the dry-land operation in Lind as well, and part of the workforce from Espanola commuted back and forth every day.[75] In the interest of productivity, the group sold the 400-acre, irrigated farm in the late winter of 1963,[76] and concentrated their efforts on the dry-land farming of wheat, barley and hay.[77] They added a commercial chicken raising department to the Espanola farm, an operation which had been a successful component of Pincher Creek Colony. But the chickens and eggs recorded little profit for the colony in Washington, so they were replaced by geese, ducks, and turkeys.[78] "The chickens didn't bring in much money, only 'chicken feed'."[79] With a goose population of more than 1,000, the Hutterites became the only commercial geese raisers in Washington.[80] At any given time, "we have 300 geese in cold storage in Spokane, ready for the oven."[81]

The switch from chicken to geese production was only one of the profitable changes they made. As the colony developed, the dairy operation grew as well. The Hutterites began with a small number of cows and slowly acquired more. As milk production increased, the colony modernized by installing an automated milking carousel, making it possible to "milk eight cows in eight minutes."[82] The Brethren signed a contract with the Carnation Company in Spokane, agreeing to sell Carnation all their milk.[83] "We had 80 cows, but after a meeting with Carnation and the bank . . . we doubled the number . . ."[84] The dairy operation grew to such productive levels that it became "a half a million dollar deal."[85]

The Hutterites in the west have almost always farmed coarse grains, such as wheat, barley, and oats; the colony at Spokane was no exception. They added acreage for growing alfalfa for the dairy herd, and began taking some of their grain and alfalfa to the Fox Milling Corporation in Mead, where it was turned into pelletized cattle feed for their own herds and flocks.[86] Typical of Hutterian self-sufficiency, this was also an efficient way to feed their animals.

At some point in the 1970s, the group, always searching for profitable ventures, decided to raise commercial turf grass.

> For several years, well into the 1980s, they raised this turf grass, but it was either not profitable or it simply did not suit them for one reason or another. In time, this operation too was left by the wayside.[87]

The grass-growing operation was sold to a Portland, Oregon, firm,[88] and the Hutterites then discussed what their next venture would be. They had always grown potatoes for their own use. By the mid-1970s, they were planting sixty acres of potatoes; at thirty tons per acre, this was a relatively productive endeavor.[89] They decided to develop it, eventually adopting the seed potato as their primary product.

> The Hutterites discussed potatoes for quite some time. They researched every variant of potato tuber in the world, looking for the best class that would be most profitable to them. It was discovered that the finest seed potato to be had was found in Montana. After contacting some growers there, they sent several trucks to Montana, and brought back enough seed to commence what would become a very substantial operation.[90]

The key to the Hutterites success as farmers has been their willingness to adapt to the peculiarities of the land on which they live. The change to potato farming has been perhaps the most profitable of all the changes they have made in their years in Washington.

> Diversification is regulated by geography. Depending on the region, a colony grows what's best for that region. In our case, the best so far has been the seed potato. Idaho may be home of famous potatoes, but Washington soil grows the finest . . .[91]

Gründliche kurtz verfaste Historia.

**Von Münsterischen Wi-**
dertäuffern: vnd wie die Hutterischen Brüder
so auch billich Widertäuffer genent werden / im Löblichen
Marggraffthumb Mährern / deren aber die sibentzeben tausent sein
sollen/gedachten Münsterischen in vilen ähnlich/
gleichformig vnd mit zustimmet sein.

Durch.
Christoffen Erhard Theologum, auf der Fürstlichen
Graffschafft Tyrol/von Hall geborn.

Gedruckt zu München/bey Adam Berg.
Cum gratia & priuilegio Cæf: May:
Anno M. D. LXXXVIIII.

Tracht der Hutterer im 16. Jahrhundert.

**1.** (left) Sixteenth century woodcut, depicting the styles of dress and the design of the bruderhofs of early Hutterites (photo courtesy of Spokane Hutterian Brethren [SHB]).

**2.** (below) Pincher Creek Colony, Alberta, shortly after its founding in 1926 (photo courtesy of SHB).

**3.** (bottom) Wolf Creek Colony, site of the first Dariusleut community in North America, showing the standard layout of a typical modern Hutterite colony (photo courtesy of Lawrence Anderson).

4. (above) Harvesting at Pincher Creek Colony with the first three self-propelled combines manufactured by Massey Harris (photo by Lorena Bach).

5. (left) William Gross, manager of the Spokane Hutterian Brethren (photo courtesy of SHB).

6. (below) A timeless scene of Hutterite life at Spokane Colony. (photo courtesy of SHB).

7. (above right) Women in the garden at Pincher Creek Colony, in the 1940s (photo courtesy of SHB).

8. (below right) Hutterites in traditional dress seem anachronistic amid the modern farm buildings of Spokane Colony (photo courtesy of SHB).

**9.** (left) Paul S. Gross, the farmer (photo courtesy of SHB).
**10.** (above) Paul S. Gross, the trapper (photo courtesy of SHB).
**11.** (below) Paul S. Gross, the historian (photo courtesy of SHB).
**12.** (above right) The farm in Lind, which the Hutterites leased in 1956 (photo courtesy of SHB).
**13.** (right) Spokane Colony, shortly after it was built, circa 1961 (photo courtesy of SHB).
**14.** (below right) Spokane Colony, three decades later. The community, as well as the shade trees, have flourished (photo courtesy of the author).

**15.** (left) A sampling of antique Hutterite books still in use (photo courtesy of SHB).

**16.** (above) As in many Hutterite communities, the schoolhouse at Spokane Colony doubles as a church. Here a family enters the schoolhouse for evening services (photo courtesy of SHB).

**17.** (below) The future leaders and followers of the Spokane Hutterian Brethren. How will they fare in the 21st century (photo courtesy of SHB)?

**18.** (above right) Always the teacher, Paul S. Gross draws the attention of his young audience to one of the many newspapers to which the colony subscribes (photo courtesy of The Seattle Times).

**19.** (below) The intellectual legacy continues: grandson Phillip Gross listens as Paul S. Gross, semi-retired, reads from *The Hutterite Way* (photo courtesy of SHB).

**20.** Mothers and children of the Spokane Hutterian Brethren in a moment of relaxation (photo courtesy of SHB).

The development of these various agricultural ventures, combined with the modest orchard, the five-acre garden, and the numerous farm and shop implements they manufactured, served to successfully establish the Hutterians in Washington.

The number of people of the colony grew as well. Sixty people comprised the community's membership when it was first formed.[92] Demographic studies indicate that approximately fifteen to twenty years pass before a colony's population doubles.[93] "By 1972, we were about close to 100."[94] Colony records show approximately thirty people were born in Washington between 1956 and 1972,[95] and seven women were added to the population through marriage.[96] The growth rate of the Spokane Hutterian Brethren during this period was countered by few deaths. On Sunday, April 1, 1967, Paul's wife, Sarah, died and was interred in the colony's small, private cemetery.[97]

Though many Hutterian colonies do not branch until a maximum population has been accommodated, the Dariusleut "are more willing to form new colonies sooner, and do not mind starting out with a small labor force and marginal resources."[98] For twelve years the Spokane group had commuted from the colony to farm the land near Lind. In 1972, they decided to branch.

> We branched prematurely. We had a pretty big opera-
> tion down there and we tried to run it from here. It was
> a real hassle though, so we branched early. If we had
> waited until the typical colony size of between 120 and
> 150 was reached, we'd be splitting up about now.[99]

The number of people was smaller than usual, but the success of the farm provided for substantial financial resources.

> When they decided to split in the traditional manner, we
> spent many long hours pouring over the assets. Finally
> we were able to reach an agreement which was satisfac-
> tory to all of the membership and both parties came
> away from the split with a very comfortable amount of
> capital.[100]

The Wollman families, accompanied by several Gross families, departed from Espanola and established the Warden Hutterian Brethren,

Inc., "in Big Bend Electric Co-op territory about 25 miles east of Moses Lake."[101] This left a relatively small group of Hutterian Brethren in Spokane County to work their 3,600-acre farm, while the new colony at Warden formally took over a 10,000-acre operation.[102]

Espanola Colony,[103] now known as Spokane Colony, easily rose to the challenge of farming their land with a diminished labor pool. The colony has prospered in the ensuing years, acquiring more land, which presently totals approximately 5,600 acres. Half the farm is irrigated, and the rest is dry-land. They continue to raise seed potatoes as their main product, harvesting bumper crops year after year. It seems that their traditional stewardship of the land will continue in Washington for many years to come.

The colony currently has fifty-two members, including families with children, a childless marriage, and several widows and unmarried women (see Appendix A, page 109).[104] Although it is an essentially endogamous community, it is not completely closed. In the autumn of 1986, a young neighbor named Steve Benning began living at the colony, with the aspiration of becoming a Hutterite.[105]

> I've known them for years . . . I've always felt they had something very special here – the way everyone works together, the way the whole colony is like a big, close-knit family. It's what I want.[106]

Benning spent five years working for the corporation and learning German. He was committed in his desire for formal conversion to the Hutterite faith, and underwent seven weeks of intensive religious instruction. The Hutterite ministers[107] instructed him in English, in order to be certain he understood the seriousness of his decision to join the colony.[108] Steve Benning was baptized on Sunday, April 8, 1990, and married Joanne Gross in late 1991.[109]

This acceptance of an outsider into their midst[110] is an example of the increasingly friendly relationship which has finally begun to develop between the Hutterites and their neighbors.

> . . . early suspicions about the Hutterites have been allayed as friendships developed. A "comfortable" relationship has been worked out . . . And now the

neighbors accept them, more or less satisfied to let the Hutterites live as they feel they should.[111]

Paul Gross feels that moving to Washington has been one of the wisest decisions he has made in his long life.

> I dearly love it here. The people are friendly and, on the average, spiritually minded. The land has been good to us and we've been good to the land. The climate is wonderful too. When we get visitors from Alberta, I always ask them, "Has the wind stopped blowing yet?" Yes, Washington has been like a promised land for us.[112]

Besides the Spokane and Warden colonies, Washington has become home to two other fully-established colonies: Stahlville, near Ritzville, and Marlin, near Ruff. Additionally, two much smaller communities have been attempting to establish themselves near Odessa. Only time will tell if they will be successful; perhaps they will be able to call Washington their "promised land" as well.

# NOTES

1.  John Hostetler, *Hutterite Society*, (Baltimore: The Johns Hopkins University Press, 1974), 185.

2.  Paul Gross, interview with the author, November 23, 1991.

3.  Gross, interview with the author, November 23, 1991.

4.  Gross, interview with the author, November 23, 1991. The entire Hutterite delegation to Mexico comprised members from several Alberta colonies, not just Pincher Creek.

5.  Gross, interview with the author, November 23, 1991.

6.  Gross, interview with the author, November 23, 1991.

7.  Gross, interview with the author, November 23, 1991.

8.      Gross, interview with the author, November 23, 1991.

9.      Gross, interview with the author, November 23, 1991.

10.      Gross, interview with the author, November 23, 1991. The name of this man was not disclosed through the course of several interviews with Paul Gross.

11.      Gross, interview with the author, November 23, 1991.

12.      Paul S. Gross, "The Geographical Expansian [sic] of the Hutterite Colonies" (unpublished address, National Historic Communal Societies Association, Yankton, South Dakota, October 6, 1989), 2.

13.      Gross, interview with the author, April 4, 1992.

14.      Paul Gross in Michael Schmeltzer, "Hutterites: A People Apart," *Washington*, III (March-April, 1987), 65. The full story was pursued after reading this particular article. Paul's great-uncle, during his journey, also herded sheep in Oregon.

15.      Gross, interview with the author, November 23, 1991.

16.      Gross, interview with the author, November 23, 1991.

17.      Gross, interview with the author, November 23, 1991. "Clarence was no Mennonite though." Ibid.

18.      Gross, interview with the author, November 23, 1991.

19.      Gross, "Geographical Expansian [sic]" 2. The tract of land in question was the estate of the late John L. Fox. Mrs. Hagen was Fox's daughter; thus Clarence held the land in trust.

20.      Gross, "Geographical Expansian [sic]," 2.

21.      Gross, "Geographical Expansian [sic]," 3.

22.      Gross, "Geographical Expansian [sic]," 3. Paul corroborated this in the interview of November 15, 1991.

23.      Jansen was a partner in the Ritzville law firm of Miller, Miller & Jansen. He was born in Lind, Washington, in 1917, of pioneer parents who came to Washington Territory in 1889, shortly before statehood. He studied for his degree of juris doctor at Columbia Law School, and was a protégé of Justice William O. Douglas of the United States Supreme Court. It was

Douglas who talked Jansen into moving back to Lind. Jansen began practicing law in Ritzville in 1951.

24. Leonard F. Jansen, retired attorney, Spokane, Washington, personal interview with the author at his home, April 8, 1992. Jansen represented all of the Dariusleut in Washington until his retirement in 1991.

25. Paul S. Gross, "Hutterite Colony Finds New Acceptance, Opportunity in U.S.," *Mennonite Weekly Review*, (June 29, 1967), 9.

26. *The Spokesman-Review*, 10 August 1956. The Hutterites purchased most of Hagen's machinery as well.

27. Gross, "New Acceptance," 9.

28. Sandra K. McAvory, "The Hutterites; An Unusually Modern Old-fashioned People," *Ruralite*, (August, 1973), 8. The quote is from Jacob Wollman, Jr., who was part of the initial move to Washington in 1956.

29. "The Promised Land," *Time*, (August 13, 1956), 26.

30. "The Promised Land," *Time*, (August 13, 1956), 26.

31. *The Spokesman-Review*, 10 August 1956.

32. "The Promised Land," *Time*, (August 13, 1956), 26.

33. Gross, interview with the author, November 15, 1991.

34. Draftees who were conscientious objectors during World War II served instead with the Forest Service, the Red Cross, and (the Hutterites specifically) at Custer Federal Game Park and in the Black Hills of South Dakota. See Paul S. Gross, *The Hutterite Way* (Saskatoon: Freeman Publishing Company, Ltd., 1965), 124-127.

35. Jansen, interview with the author, April 8, 1992.

36. Gross, "New Acceptance," 9.

37. Gross, "New Acceptance," 9.

38. Gross, interview with the author, November 15, 1991.

39. It must be remembered that the Hagen dryland was leased to the Hutterites.

40. Jansen, interview with the author, April 8, 1992.

41. Gross, "New Acceptance," 9. Approximately 1,500 acres, or half of their Spokane holdings, were purchased from Alvin Brende.
42. Revised Code of Washington 1881, ch. 24.08, sect. .025, 138-139.
43. *Spokane Daily Chronicle*, 27 June 1961.
44. *Spokane Daily Chronicle*, 27 June 1961.
45. Paul S. Gross, *Pincher Creek Colony: Memories* (Pincher Creek, ALTA: By the author, n.d.), 35.
46. Gross, interview with the author, May 2, 1992.
47. Stan Sloan, Building Contractor, Bestway Building Supply, Spokane, Washington, interview with the author at his home, Spokane, Washington, March 7, 1992.
48. Sloan, interview with the author, March 7, 1992.
49. Gross, interview with the author, November 15, 1991.
50. Sloan, interview with the author, March 7, 1992.
51. Gross, "New Acceptance," 9.
52. *Spokane Daily Chronicle*, 27 June 1961. The colony was fairly complete by the summer of 1961. Subsequent structures were erected as the need for them arose.
53. *Spokesman-Review*, 1 July 1960.
54. Sloan, interview with the author, March 7, 1992.
55. *Spokane Daily Chronicle*, 27 June 1961.
56. *Spokesman-Review*, 27 May 1962.
57. Jansen, interview with the author, April 8, 1992.
58. *Spokesman-Review*, 27 May 1962.
59. *Spokesman-Review*, 27 May 1962.
60. Jansen, interview with the author, April 8, 1992. The exact nature of these rumors and the literature, (presumably simple leaflets), has faded over the course of thirty years. It may be supposed that much of the slander revolved around the aura of McCarthyism which still pervaded much of American society at the time.

61. *Spokesman-Review*, 27 May 1962.

62. *Spokesman-Review*, 27 May 1962. The Hutterian Brethren of Spokane owned 1,500 acres of land at this time.

63. Sarah Anne Gross, granddaughter of Paul Gross, Spokane Colony, informal interview with the author at her home, Spokane Hutterian Brethren, Inc., May 2, 1992. It is fairly easy, once an outsider is considered non-threatening, to converse freely with the Dariusleut women at Spokane. I have spent many hours in conversation with individual members of the Gross family. Several sessions were undertaken with Sarah alone; Paul has, on numerous occasions when he was busy with other matters, said to me: "Go ask Sarah Anne; she knows as much as I do."

64. *Spokesman-Review*, 27 May 1962.

65. *Spokesman-Review*, 27 May 1962.

66. *Spokesman-Review*, 27 May 1962.

67. The Hutterian Brethren are a fully religious manifestation. In view of this historical fact, the Hutterian Brethren of Spokane receive, as do all Hutterite corporations, only the tax concessions which are lawfully given to religious corporations; they pay all taxes to which they are obligated; colonies combine all individual tax forms and pay a single, corporate income tax. As a religious corporation, property where religious services are held is accorded exemption status for tax purposes. Consequently, only about half an acre at Spokane is exempt (see section 501[b] of the IRS code).

68. *Spokesman-Review*, 27 May 1962. Though the Hutterites migrated to America from Russia, they have no Russian "background" whatsoever. During their century-long tenure in the Ukraine, they received no converts from the local populace. The same holds true for their earlier periods of establishment in Moravia, Wallachia and Transylvania; they have always been composed entirely of Germanic families.

69. *Spokesman-Review*, 27 May 1962.

70. *Spokesman-Review*, 27 May 1962.

71. Jansen, interview with the author, April 8, 1992.

72 *Spokesman-Review*, 17 June 1962.

73. Jansen, interview with the author, April 8, 1992.

74. Gross, "New Acceptance," 9.

75. William (Bill) Gross, Manager, Spokane Hutterian Brethren, Inc., telephone interview with the author, October 12, 1991.

76. *Spokane Daily Chronicle*, 9 March 1963.

77. Paul Gross, interview with the author, May 2, 1992.

78. *Spokane Daily Chronicle*, 16 November 1977.

79. Sarah Anne Gross, interview with the author, May 2, 1992.

80. *Spokesman-Review*, 10 December 1983.

81. *Spokane Daily Chronicle*, 16 November 1977. The ducks and turkeys are a lesser component of the poultry operation; nonetheless the colony produces hundreds of these birds as well.

82. *Spokane Daily Chronicle*, 16 November 1977.

83. *Spokane Daily Chronicle*, 16 November 1977. The colony still maintains this contract with Carnation.

84. *Spokane Daily Chronicle*, 16 November 1977.

85. Paul Gross in *Spokane Daily Chronicle*, 16 November 1977.

86. *Spokane Daily Chronicle*, 16 November 1977.

87. Jansen, interview with the author, April 8, 1992.

88. Paul Gross, interview with the author, May 2, 1992. "That was about seven years ago." Ibid. Paul was not too specific as to when this occurred, but the sale took place in the mid-1980s, probably 1984, according to Sarah Anne Gross, interview with the author, May 2,1982.

89. *Spokane Daily Chronicle*, 16 November 1977.

90. Jansen, interview with the author, April 8, 1992.

91. Bill Gross, interview with the author, November 7, 1991.

92. Paul Gross, interview with the author, May 2, 1992.

93. John Bennett, *Hutterian Brethren*, (Stanford: Stanford University Press, 1967), 181.

94. Paul Gross, interview with the author, November 23, 1991.

95. *Dariusleut Colony Genealogies*: Colony #46 – Espanola, 1-5, Colony #78 – Warden, 1-9.

96. *Dariusleut Colony Genealogies*: Colony #46 – Espanola, 1-5, Colony #78 – Warden, 1-9.

97. *Spokesman-Review*, 2 April 1967.

98. Bennett, *Hutterian Brethren*, 182.

99. Bill Gross, interview with the author, October 20, 1991.

100. Jansen, interview with the author, April 8, 1992.

101. McAvory, "The Hutterites," 6.

102. McAvory, "The Hutterites," 7.

103. The colony in Spokane County has been known by several names: Espanola Colony, Deep Creek Colony, Reardan Colony. The reasons for the various appellations are attributable to the location of the colony grounds. The communities of Espanola and Deep Creek lie in close proximity to the Hutterites, and their mailing address, which in 1964 was Rural Route 1, Box 49, Espanola, WA 99010, was switched in 1973 to Rural Route 1, Box 6-E, Reardan, WA 99029, even though Reardan is in Lincoln County. The name of the corporation was also changed from *The Hutterian Brethren of Spokane, Inc*, to *Spokane Hutterian Brethren, Inc*.

104. Sarah Anne Gross, interview with the author, October 7, 1994. At the request of the author, Sarah conducted a census of the colony and compiled a table of data which contained the names of the members, along with dates of births, marriages, baptisms, and deaths. For the purpose of simplification, only the names of the living members are given (see Appendix A, page 109).

105. Michael Schmeltzer, "Hutterites: A People Apart," *Washington*, III (March-April,1987), 66.

106. Schmeltzer, "Hutterites," 66.

107. Paul Gross is the minister and Samuel Gross is the second or assistant minister.

108. Paul Gross, interview with the author, November 23, 1991.

109.    Sarah Anne Gross, *Spokane Hutterian Census*, February, 1992.

110.    Steve Benning is the only outsider to convert at the Spokane Colony. This is not unique, but it is not common either. The absolute adherence to the communal and religious tenets of the Hutterian Brethren is extremely difficult for "people of the world" to adapt to. More common, actually, are the small numbers of Hutterites, mostly men, who leave the communal life. The majority of them return after a short time of "trying the world," but some of them seem to leave for good. One such man, Frank Gross (Paul's son) left the colony twenty-five years ago and lives in British Columbia. But kinship ties are strong, even for those who leave; Frank visits the colony periodically, when he comes to Spokane to shop. Even after such a long period of time, should Frank decide to return to communal life, he will be received with much joy.

111.    *Spokane Daily Chronicle*, 9 November 1977.

112.    Interview with the author, May 2, 1992.

*Chapter 6*

# THE INTELLECTUAL LEGACY

Since the beginning of the Anabaptist movement, the Hutterian Brethren have produced a variety of literary works. However, since the movement was heavily persecuted throughout Europe, its written records are scarce and widely scattered.[1] "Hutterite accounts about themselves and their traditions were, of course, highly sympathetic interpretations."[2] Their literature in its many forms served to insulate their members from the polemical writings of the state churches, which they considered abominable.

During the "golden years" in Moravia, the Hutterian Brethren maintained an orderly archive

> . . . where all material of significance was collected, incoming and outgoing epistles, official writings, doctrinal statements, records about martyrs, records about the brotherhood itself, notes on weather, on prices of farm products, regulations (Ordnungen), speeches of elders, and all the rest.[3]

At some point during the late 1500s, the idea of collecting this material into an official chronicle arose.[4] A succession of scribes compiled an exhaustive account of events into the *Great Chronicle*. The first chapter of the *Chronicle* is an account of recorded history up to the Reformation. The rest of the book records Hutterian history, in great detail, from the beginnings of Anabaptism (circa 1525) to 1665. The existence of an original volume of this book is miraculous, given the extreme persecutions, complete with book confiscations, that the Hutterites suffered in Europe. The *Chronicle* is a great treasure, for it has preserved the only original account of the Hutterites' early history.[5]

The archive in Moravia probably also contained an earlier work, by Peter Ridemann, the *Rechenschaft*. Known in English as the *Account of Our Religion, Doctrine, and Faith*, or *Confession of Faith*, this book was written by Ridemann "in the dry summer of 1540 as he lay a prisoner in Hesse."[6] The *Confession* was written as a formal apology for Hutterian doctrine, containing an exhaustive defense of Hutterian practices, and supported by nearly 1,800 biblical references.[7] It was well-known throughout Europe, and was one of the few Hutterite books of that time to have been published.[8] The *Rechenschaft* was apparently written for the benefit of outsiders, in order to inform them "about the true Anabaptist doctrine."[9] Nevertheless, it was considered by the Hutterian Brethren to be a flawless treatise on their beliefs, and has been adopted by Hutterites through the centuries as the central work concerning their faith.

In the period of spiritual decay, brought about primarily by the Thirty Years War, a man named Andreas Ehrenpreis was unanimously elected bishop.[10] He was "the last outstanding leader of the brotherhood during a period of decline aggressively active in a restoration of the old spirit."[11] In an effort to revive the original essence of Hutterianism, he wrote vast numbers of regulations, epistles, and doctrinal tracts designed to unify his people temporally and spiritually. Perhaps his most recognized writing is the *Sendbrief* of 1652.[12] A spiritual admonishment to the brethren, the *Sendbrief* valiantly defends the tenet of "community of goods," citing supportive biblical references.

> This *Sendbrief* is certainly no theological tract, and yet it is one of the strongest and finest products of the Hutterite spirit concerning "brotherly communion, the highest commandment of love."[13]

In spite of persecutions which almost eradicated them, and through repeated migrations, the Hutterian Brethren have managed to endure. They have been sustained by their absolute devotion to their faith and their obedience to their elders. One leading elder was Johannes Waldner, bishop of the Hutterian Brethren in the early 1800s. Waldner's family was among the Carinthian Lutherans who were expelled from Austria, arriving in Transylvania in 1755. The Carinthian merger with the Hutterites served to revitalize the movement at a time when it was in danger of dissipating. Waldner, "a zealous convert to the faith,"[14] contributed to the revitalization through his writing. He

> helped save the Hutterian movement both in Romania and the Ukraine, in part by reestablishing the tradition of chronicling Hutterian history – in itself a sign of religious renewal and firm dedication.[15]

The *Small Chronicle*, which Waldner wrote, summarized the earlier *Great Chronicle* and then proceeded to detail Hutterian history from 1665 to 1802. Subsequent contributors to the book brought the *Small Chronicle* to its conclusion in 1947.[16] Waldner included personal experiences in this work, enriching history "with a unique skill in making events live."[17]

After the Hutterites came to America, an elder of the Dariusleut, Elias Walter, rose to prominence. He was "a man of the greatest dedication to a revival of the old, genuine Hutterite spirit."[18] Continuing the literary tradition of his predecessors, Elias Walter

> . . . gathered manuscripts and codices from every possible source, and from the age of eighteen showed his gift for writing and publishing. He became one of our leading historians and spared no time or money in collecting, printing and distributing our literature. He saw that this was placed in the home of every member of the three groups. This gave the Hutterite movement a needed "shot in the arm" in America and is one of the reasons for our survival today.[19]

Historical chronicles, confessions of faith, and epistles of various kinds have all served to unify the Hutterian Brethren. The works of the writers mentioned here are examples, not only of the power of literature to sustain people's faith, but also of the depth of religious conviction which has characterized the Brethren throughout their history.

Hutterite religion is most clearly understood through sermons. Nearly all existing Hutterite sermons were written during the Ehrenpreis era, dating from 1665 or earlier.[20] The Hutterites consider these sermons "the spiritual life of the brotherhood; the food of the soul; so perfect that no one could improve upon them."[21] Exactly how many are extant is uncertain. The first duty of an elected minister is to hand copy, from the collection of the preceding minister, enough sermons to read throughout the year. As a result, sermon collections vary from one group to another. Leafing through sermon books in the solitude of Paul Gross's office, one is reminded of the illuminated volumes of Christian antiquity; their gothic calligraphy gives them the appearance of being quite old. "Due to the uncompromising Biblicism of all sermons, they call their reading 'sharp preaching,' in contrast to the soft preaching in other churches."[22] This use of historical sermons is another expression of the Hutterites' uniqueness as a religious group (see Appendix G, page 121).

The visitor to the Spokane Colony, whether familiar with the Hutterites or not, would not immediately notice that it is unique among Hutterian communities. Certainly their communal lifestyle and their visible appearance are different from conventional society, but these, along with their cooperative agrarian pursuits, are common Hutterian characteristics. To the casual observer, all Hutterites and their communities are more or less indistinguishable from one another.

A closer look, however, reveals a cultural self-confidence which sets Spokane quite apart. This dynamic atmosphere is directly attributable to Paul Gross. As minister for the community, he serves as counselor, spiritual leader, mediator, and advocate for his people in "the world."[23] These are the functions all Hutterian ministers perform for their communities. But there is an extraordinary quality about Paul. His granddaughter, Sarah Anne Gross, explains:

> Grandpa has always been different from other elders. It's hard to explain; he puts much value in education, but it has to be the "right" education. Much of what is taught in the schools of the world is useless to us. What is important is that we completely understand our place in history. Grandpa, with his brains, his books, and his education, separates what is of value and has taught it to us.[24]

The particular qualities which set Paul Gross apart from his counterparts, and which in turn set the Spokane community apart from other colonies, are his determination, his sharp intellect, and his unwillingness to compromise.

> He speaks his mind. He only says what he feels is right – and he is very wise. As an example, if something sitting on a shelf were white, so obviously white, and some clever man came in and proceeded to speak so persuasively saying that the thing was black, after sometime he will have convinced many people that it was indeed black. But Grandpa, even if he were the last man in the world left unconvinced, would not stray from his convictions. After all, the thing was white.[25]

This independence of mind, already apparent in Paul when he advocated moving to Washington, exemplifies the confidence with which all the Spokane Hutterian Brethren approach life. Even the younger members are encouraged to have a bold approach to enquiry.

> We have been brought up with what is believed to be truth; we know what is right and what is wrong. But we are allowed to speak our minds too. We may get in trouble for it – we understand that – but nevertheless, we are able to say what we feel. Not all my girlfriends can say that.[26]

Over half a century ago, when Paul Gross became German school teacher, and then minister, he commenced a life of scholarship, as had so many Hutterian ministers before him. His early writing consisted mostly of the copying of sermons, but his skill as a writer, combined with his love for history, soon led him to research and writing about many aspects of Hutterianism.

While still living in Pincher Creek, Paul began a regular correspondence with Dr. Robert Friedmann, the foremost Anabaptist scholar in America. For over fifteen years, they exchanged ideas and research notes.[27] In addition to translating a variety of Hutterian literature into English, Paul published numerous pamphlets on religious, secular, and historical themes. These were significant in that they were available for distribution to the outside world.[28] The promotion of Hutterianism to the larger society was not a missionary activity per se, although it certainly had this capability. Rather, Paul was conscious of the vast amount of misinformation regarding the Hutterites, and strongly desired to correct misconceptions about them through his writing.

The enactment of the Communal Property Act brought an increased awareness of Hutterian existence to the people of Canada and the United States. When the Hutterites decided to venture out of Alberta in the 1950s, they created quite a stir.

> When the editors of the *Lethbridge Herald* heard about
> it they were on my place and wanted to know the facts.
> Well, facts they got. Then it spread from one newspaper
> to another: *The Wall Street Journal*, *Edmonton Journal*,
> *Vancouver Sun*, *Time Magazine*, which covered the
> story with pictures, together with all Canadian maga-
> zines. The radios blared. I hardly had any rest.[29]

Their new migration caused "such a public interest that I received a number of letters of varying kinds from different people."[30] The multitude of inquiries came from individuals with a variety of interests. Many had heard of the Hutterites through the newspapers and magazines and wondered who they were. Others wanted to sell their farms to them, and still others wanted Hutterite literature about their religious beliefs.[31] While the newly-formed colony at Spokane attempted to accommodate people's requests to visit it, Paul felt the need to produce a written work which would answer the questions he was being asked.

> The earnest questions of serious seekers after truth have
> given me cause to write a more comprehensive and
> clear description of the character of Hutterite communal
> life, in its spiritual and religious aspects as well as from
> an economic point of view, for we are an economic
> entity . . .[32]

Published in 1965,[33] *The Hutterite Way* was the first complete treatise on Hutterianism ever to be written in English.[34] It was also the first book containing photographs of the Hutterian people.

> For nearly five centuries it has not been possible to publish a pictorial book about the Hutterites, apart from the occasional newspaper article which had a photograph or two added.[35]

Since posing for pictures goes against Hutterian principles, the photographs used in the book were candid. Even so, Paul had to get authorization from the elders in Alberta to include the pictures in his book.[36] Several of the elders resisted, much as they had resisted Paul's move to Washington. It was not an easy task for Paul to convince his brethren. His argument, however, was convincing:

> It has long been my feeling that the truth could be advanced and broadcast by publishing a few educational and interesting pictures about the colonies. There are such pictures in the Bible, and we accept that these imaginary pictures elucidate the story.[37]

In the end, he obtained a reluctant authorization.[38]

The book was an immediate success. It was widely promoted by the publisher to libraries of all kinds and to booksellers. Paul Gross promoted the book personally as well, and saw that it went to most of the Hutterite colonies in North America, as well as to several libraries in Europe.[39]

While *The Hutterite Way* is, naturally, a sympathetic interpretation of Hutterianism, it is not a polemic; it is written in an informal manner, with great candor, the way Paul Gross speaks. And, like earlier Hutterian works, it contains extensive biblical references (see Appendix B, page 110). Earlier works on Hutterianism, except Peter Ridemann's *Rechenschaft*, were written primarily for Hutterites. Paul Gross' book, on the other hand, offers a window through which outsiders may see Hutterian life. It is this departure from Hutterian tradition which sets Paul Gross and his community apart.

Paul Gross has been a prolific writer, accumulating an extensive bibliography while maturing into a world-renowned Hutterian scholar.[40]

In addition, he has published much of his own work, as well as works written in many other Hutterite colonies in North America.[41] Thus, the tools of Paul's trade are "quite different from those used in other aspects of the [colony's] operation."[42]

Paul Gross' writing holds a significant place in the field of Hutterian history. While most literature in the field is authored by academics, these writers invariably cite Paul's work among their sources.

> I would think that anything Paul Gross has written (and it is considerable) would be genuinely part of the primary source materials for your purposes. Paul Gross is *the* historian of his generation, among the Hutterites, who has dared to interpret Hutterian history, early and more recent.[43]

## Paul Gross – Later Years

During the early years in Washington, Paul made time for writing, ministering, and farm work in his busy schedule. He also travelled a great deal, both as a historian and as a minister. He went to Europe three times, to consult archives, libraries, and museums, and to visit the places in Eastern Europe where his ancestors had experienced prosperity and growth, and persecution and decline.[44] His emergence as an authority on Hutterianism led him on lecture tours to several colleges and universities, and to various societal gatherings.[45] And his wisdom has been called upon numerous times by his brethren, both in the United States and in Canada, to help settle matters of dispute.

Paul Gross is now 85 years old. Over the years, as he became less involved in the farming operation, he devoted more of his time to writing. His health declined; he had bypass surgery and several hospitalizations, and in 1978 he developed hemochromatosis.[46] This little-known condition debilitates a person by dramatically increasing the level of iron in the blood. In spite of advances in medical technology, the only effective remedy is bleeding; Paul must undergo semi-monthly phlebotomies.[47]

In 1993, Paul developed pneumonia, which further weakened him. He is now more or less fully retired from active life, though he still "keeps his hand in." His inner strength far outweighs his physical strength, and he remains a vibrant member of his community.

> I'm not pressed to do anything outside of my writing in my later twenty years; it's my free will, because I'm a minister. I write, eat, sleep, preach, visit other colonies, give advice to those who seek it, and then I write some more.[48]

There is a place for everyone in a Hutterian community; Paul's place is where he chooses it to be:

> Old age is no reason not to work . . . Maybe I'm not out there digging potatoes, but I keep busy. We all have jobs to do. That's the way we live.[49]

When Paul discusses topics of interest, he often says, in his raspy yet gentle voice: "I've got something about that written down somewhere. I'll just go get it."[50] Then this soft-spoken man, dressed in dark trousers, suspenders, plain shirt buttoned to the top, and soft slippers, rises slowly – he does few things quickly – and shuffles into the darkened room at the rear of the house. "If you'll come in here you'll see that I'm just plainly overcrowded."[51] I follow, eager to glimpse the private life of these fascinating people. He takes in the whole room with a sweep of his hand; stacks of books lie all about, dwarfed by piles of unbound manuscript material in no apparent order. In this confusion of paperwork, Paul always finds what he is looking for. His capacity for detail is admirable indeed, and recognized by all who know him.

As a minister, a teacher, and a writer, Paul Gross has worked effectively to integrate aspects of contemporary life into the historical culture of the Hutterian Brethren. He has also used his gift for writing to reveal the tenets of Hutterian faith to the world at large, in the hope that this will foster increased mutual understanding.

> If we are to understand the world and our own lives we must refer to the lessons of past history. Every age must rewrite its own past. More so than any other, our age

has forgotten the lessons of the past . . . There never was a time when the Hutterites needed publicity or assistance from the world . . . and they do not specifically need any such publicity now, but the world needs the peace which we have found.[52]

# NOTES

1.  Robert Friedmann, "The Epistles of the Hutterite Brethren," *Mennonite Quarterly Review*, XX (1946) 147-177. (Reprinted in Robert Friedmann, *Hutterite Studies* (Goshen, IN: Mennonite Historical Society, 1961), 157).

2.  Leonard Gross, *The Golden Years of the Hutterites* (Scottsdale, PA: Herald Press, 1980), 37.

3.  Friedmann, "Hutterite Chronicles," *Mennonite Encyclopedia*, I (1955), 589-591 (Reprinted in Friedmann, *Hutterite Studies*, 151).

4.  Friedmann, *Hutterite Studies*, 151.

5   Fortunately, the *Great Chronicle* has been translated into English and has been an invaluable primary source for this research. It contains a martyrology of over 2000 names which, combined with its historical worth, impresses on the mind of the reader the profound essence of the early Hutterian experience.

6.  The quote is from a marginal note by Dr. Rudolf Wolkan, in his edition of the *Great Chronicle* (Vienna, 1923), 167, as noted in "Peter Ridemann and the Hutterian Movement up to the Present Time," (Appendix I) in Ridemann, *Confession of Faith* (London: Hodder & Stoughton; Rifton, NY: Plough Publishing House, 1950), 269. The English translation edition of the *Chronicle* (Rifton, NY: Plough Publishing House, 1987), contains the same marginal note on page 200. According to

Friedmann, *Hutterite Studies*, 266-267, Ridemann's imprison-
ment lasted until 1542.

7.    The great amount of scriptural references were essentially
footnotes. In the translated edition (1950) listed in this bibliography, these citations are compiled as an appendix, in endnote
form, which totals thirty-seven pages. The German Bible which
Ridemann used was the *Froschauer* version, originally a reprint
of Martin Luther's translation. The *Froschauer Bible*, however,
contained an altered word order and vocabulary; until 1525, this
version was permeated with Swiss vocalizations and only later
did New High German speech patterns enter into its text. Thus,
Ridemann's citations, when used for cross-referencing, differ
considerably from scriptural quotations in modern English
versions of the Bible, making a word-for-word comparison
quite difficult and confusing. See "Froschauer Bibles and Testa-
ments," *Mennonite Encyclopedia*, I (1956), 415-416. (*Mennonite
Encyclopedia* hereinafter cited as *M.E.*).

8.    The *Rechenschaft* was published in 1565. The last page of the
published work says: "This year the *Confession* was reprinted
by Philips Vollanndt." Nothing, however, is known of this
printer. See Friedmann, "Peter Ridemann's Rechenschaft,"
*Hutterite Studies*, 224-228.

9.    Friedmann, "Peter Ridemann's Rechenschaft," *Hutterite Studies*,
224.

10.   *The Chronicle of the Hutterian Brethren* (Rifton, NY: Plough
Publishing House, 1987), 736. Ehrenpreis's election to the
position of elder took place on October 4, 1639.

11.   *M.E.*, I. 165.

12.   *M.E.*, I. 165. The *Sendbrief* was also printed.

13.   *M.E.*, I. 166.

14.   David Flint, *The Hutterites: A Study in Prejudice* (Toronto:
Oxford University Press, 1975), 75.

15.   Leonard Gross, *The Golden Years*, 212.

16.   Friedmann, "Johannes Waldner," *Hutterite Studies*, 282. The
Hutterites are planning a third *Chronicle* which would treat

their history from 1947 to the present. Paul Gross is playing an important part in this enterprise.

17. Friedmann, "Johannes Waldner," *Hutterite Studies*, 282.

18. Friedmann, "Elias Walter," *Hutterite Studies*, 283.

19. Paul S. Gross, *The Hutterite Way*, (Saskatoon: Freeman Publishing Company. 1965), 187.

20. M.E., IV, 504. There were many sermon writers, some anonymous, others known by name, chief of which was Andreas Ehrenpreis himself. Ibid., 504, 505. Sermon writing has recently become accepted again, so there are now a few modern sermons in use.

21. *Sermon Directory of the Hutterian Brethren*, (2nd edition, Reardan, WA: Spokane Hutterian Brethren, 1991), i-ii.

22. *Sermon Directory*, ii.

23. Paul Gross is also the president of the corporation.

24. Sarah Anne Gross, interview with the author at her home, May 2, 1992.

25. Sarah Anne Gross, interview with the author, May 2, 1992.

26. Sarah Anne Gross, interview with the author, May 2, 1992. Sarah refers to her friends in other colonies.

27. Robert Friedmann MSS. Archives of the Mennonite Church, Goshen, IN. Hist Mss. 1-404, General Correspondence: Box 8, Folder 16: Paul Gross, 1955-1963; Box 8, Folder 17: Paul Gross, 1964-1970. Robert Friedmann died in 1970.

28. Paul's pamphlets are small yet, extremely informative. See bibliography for a partial listing.

29. Paul Gross, "The Geographical Expansian [sic] of the Hutterite Colonies" (unpublished address, National Historic Communal Societies Association, Yankton, South Dakota, October 6,1989), 3.

30. Paul Gross, *The Hutterite Way*, xi.

31. Paul Gross, *The Hutterite Way*, xi.

32. Paul Gross, *The Hutterite Way*, xi.

33. Saskatoon: Freeman Publishing Company, Ltd.

34. Leonard Gross, archivist, Archives of the Mennonite Church, Goshen, Indiana, personal interview with the author at his home, March 19, 1992.

35. Paul Gross, *The Hutterite Way*, xii.

36. Leonard Gross, interview with the author, March 19, 1992.

37. Paul Gross, *The Hutterite Way*, xii.

38. Paul Gross, Espanola, WA, letter, 10 August 1964, to Robert Friedmann.

39. Paul Gross, interview with the author, November 15, 1991.

40. At this writing, Paul has not yet compiled a personal bibliography. He defends this by saying, "I'm too busy writing and translating. It would be quite a task; we'll let someone else do that." Interview with the author, March 26, 1992.

41. *Spokane Daily Chronicle*, 16 November 1977.

42. *Spokane Daily Chronicle*, 16 November 1977.

43. Leonard Gross, Goshen, IN, letter, 3 February 1992, to the author.

44. Paul Gross, interview with the author, November 15, 1991.

45. Paul Gross, interview with the author, November 15, 1991.

46. Paul Gross, interview with the author, November 15, 1991.

47. Medical professionals have, at times, wanted to use Paul (while still alive) to conduct research on hemochromatosis. So far, he has not consented.

48. Paul Gross, interview with the author, November 23, 1991.

49. *Spokesman-Review*, 14 October 1987.

50. Paul Gross, interview with the author, November 15, 1991.

51. Paul Gross, interview with the author, November 15, 1991.

52. Paul Gross, *The Hutterite Way*, xiii.

## *Chapter 7*
## CONCLUSION

The Hutterian Brethren are quite conscious of their heritage. Their collective lifestyle, as well as their literature, serve to preserve their historical culture. Theirs is a continuing story. As they approach the millennium, they will be faced with increasing pressures from modern society. The future will undoubtedly bring changes for the Hutterites, perhaps not always to their benefit. America, after all, does have a tendency to alter the fabric of its constituent subcultures. Hutterian communities are like the rest of American society insofar as they are economically driven and focused on the utilitarian. But undergirding their temporal affairs is an uncompromising faith in their interpretation of the Christian religion. As long as the Hutterites are part of the North American "melting pot," they will be challenged to maintain the inner spirituality which has sustained them for so long. There is every reason to hope that the fundamentals of their culture will endure: their strong belief in themselves, their support network of communal life, their stewardship of the land, and, most importantly, their unshakable faith in God as they see him. All these elements were present at their inception, on that day in 1528, and they continue to be the sustaining principles of Hutterianism today.

If the Hutterites are to continue their literary traditions, the older generation, fast disappearing, will have to apprentice the youth. The colony at Spokane has been a rich source of contemporary Hutterian literature. But Paul Gross's sons are already mature men involved in other matters: Frank left the community over twenty years ago, and Bill manages the entire corporation, leaving little time for historical writing. Twenty-year-old Phillip Gross, Bill's son, has demonstrated an interest in literature by systematically arranging the books for sale at the colony, and by assisting in the compilation of the *Sermon Directory of the Hutterian Brethren*. He also recently delivered Paul's sermon collection to the Archive of the Mennonite Church, and explored Amish and Mennonite culture in other parts of the country. As he finds his place in the community, perhaps he will continue the legacy of his grandfather.

## APPENDIX A

### LIST OF MEMBERS
### SPOKANE HUTTERIAN BRETHREN, INC.
### 1994

William Gross
Rachel
Danny
Sarah Anne
Rachel
Phillip
Rosanna

Paul S. Gross
Sarah Gross
Mary J. Wollman
Elizabeth
Lena
Margaret

Paul Gross
Christina
Dora
Charles
Paul
Christopher
Ted
Zachary

Jake Gross
Frieda
Conrad
Eli
Sharon
Abigail
Erik

Dan Gross
Judy
David
Peter
Lois

Sam Gross
Barbara
Sarah
Lisa
Tim
Mark

Ed Gross
Katherin
Jessica
Ruthie

Leonard Gross
Rachel
Linda
Larry

Steve Benning
Joanne
Barbara Jane

James Gross
Julia

**APPENDIX B**

Table of Contents of
**THE HUTTERITE WAY**

APPENDIX C

## A SAMPLING OF
## HUTTERIAN BRETHREN FAMILY NAMES

Hofer

Wipf

Wurz

Walter

Decker

Wollman

Tschetter

Knels

Stahl

Entz

Gross

Mandel

Waldner

Glanzer

Kleinsasser

112

## APPENDIX D

### A REPRINT OF THE YEAR A.D. 1906 ON HOW ADMISSION IS MADE TO THE HUTTERITE CHURCH AND CONGREGATION OF THE GODLY

1.The Church of Christ is the Community of the believing and the pious, the people of God, who do and have abstained from sinful life. Into this Community we are brought into true submission; that is, into the spiritual Ark of Noah, in which we can be preserved.

2.It is not a human deed, but an Act of God. Just as Mary, through faith and the Holy Spirit, conceived Christ when she placed her will in God's and said: Here I am, a servant of the Lord; be it unto me according to thy Word. Thus we must also receive Christ in faith; then He will begin and complete His Work in us.

3.(Let us be mindful) That the Church has the key and power to loose and to bind even as Christ has commanded, to put away the vicious and to receive the contrite, that it should also be binding in Heaven according to the words of Christ. Matt. 16.

4.That each should count the cost first, that will come, but one is not to counsel with flesh and blood. For they that would enter into the service of God must be prepared for tribulation for the sake of truth, and the faith, and to die for Christ's sake, if it be the will of God; be it by fire, water or the sword.

For now we have house and shelter, but we know not what will be on the morrow. Therefore, no one should join for the sake of prosperous days. He who will not be steadfast with the Godly, to suffer the evil as well as the good, and accept all as good, however the Lord may direct it, let him remain away. Whosoever does not act voluntarily, will not be forced. We desire to persuade no man with smooth words. It is not a matter of human compulsion or necessity, for God wants voluntary service. Whosoever cannot render that cheerfully and with hearty pleasure, let him remain in his former station.

5.Let no one undertake to join the Church for the sake of another; the wife for the sake of the husband, or the husband for the wife, or the children for the sake of their parents. That would be vain and building upon sand, having no permanency; but one who should build upon the rock tries to please God alone. For each must bear his own burden upon that day.

6.One must submit to and follow brotherly admonition, address, and punishment; also practice and apply the same with respect to others in the House of God, so that no one may fall into strange sins. Matt. 18:15.

7.One should submit himself in obedience to God and His Church, and not be obstinate, or do only his desire, but permit himself to be guided for the good and necessity of the Church, whithersoever it be known to be right.

8.That no one shall have any private possessions any more; for one who gives and surrenders himself to the Lord and His Church with all that he has and is able to do, as it was in the original apostolic Church, when no one said of his own possessions that they were his, but all things were common to them. This we regard as the safest way and the most perfect foundation; of this we are also assured in our hearts.

9.This we now plainly state to everyone beforehand, so that we may be under no obligations to return anything to anyone afterwards. Therefore, if anyone should undertake to join us, and later feel it impossible to remain and wish to have his returned, let him now stay away, keep his own, and leave us in peace. We are not anxious for money and possessions but only desire Godly hearts.

10.Whosoever has wrong dealings that are punishable in the world, be it that he is owing men or that he has defrauded them; or if anyone has involved himself in matters of marriage or is engaged to be married, he should first straighten these matters out. For if anyone should conceal any of these things from us and should in the meantime have himself baptized, and we should learn of these matters afterwards, such a one should be compelled to excommunicate as one who came into the Church improperly and by falsehood. Therefore, let each one be truly warned.

114

## APPENDIX E

## PETITION TO PRESIDENT WOODROW WILSON

To the Hon. Woodrow Wilson,
President of the United States,
Washington, D.C.

Our Dear President:

We, the Hutterian Brethren Church, also known as Bruderhof or Communistic Mennonites, comprising about 2,000 souls, who are living in eighteen communities in South Dakota and Montana (organized as a church since 1533), kindly appeal to you, Mr. President and your Assistants, briefly wishing to inform you of our principles and convictions regarding military service. Being men of lowly station and unversed in the ways of the world, we would ask your indulgence if in this letter we should miss the approved form.

The fundamental principles of our faith, as concerns practical life, are community of goods and non-resistance. Our community life is founded on the principle, "What is mine is thine," or in other words, on brotherly love and humble Christian service according to Acts 2:44,45: "And all that believed were together, and had all things common; and sold their possessions and goods and parted them to all men, as every man had need." Hence we differ fundamentally from non-Christian communistic systems, with their principle, "What is thine is mine." We believe the community life, if not based on Christian love, will always fail. Our endeavors are of a religious nature throughout, and we know that very few people are willing to accept our faith, denying themselves and serving God by serving each other in community life, as we do.

We are free from political ambitions and recognize civil government as ordained of God. We honor our civil authorities and in our daily evening prayer meetings, which are regularly attended by all our members, as well as in our Sunday services, we pray for our government. We have always willingly paid taxes on our real estate and personal property, although we were told that our property, being held by a religious corporation, is not taxable according to the law. It need not be said that we do not permit our widows and orphans, invalids and feeble-minded to become a burden to the county or state.

Our community life is based on God's Word, and we could not serve God according to the dictates of our consciences if we were not permitted to live together in our communities. Our members would, by the help of God, suffer what He may permit, rather than consent to leave the community life.

On the principle of non-resistance our position is strictly in accordance with the New Testament teaching. Our *Confession of Faith* shows that we hold the government to be ordained of God for the reason that not all men are followers of the meek and lowly Savior, and that we further believe, the government should protect those who do good and punish the evil-doers according to Rom. 13:1-7. The Church, however, must conform to the express teachings and examples of the Master. She is in the world, but not of the world. We have never taken any part in the election of civil officers. Without boasting we can say that our life has been consistent with this principle. To go to law is contrary to our convictions and is not permitted among us. Our young men could not become a part of the army or military organizations, even for non-combatant service, without violating our principles.

Our comprehensive *Confession of Faith* was written in 1540 and printed for the first time in 1565. The voluminous *Chronicle of our Church*, which gives our history since the year 1530, is mentioned in the article, "Mennonites" in the *International Encyclopedia*. The principal contents of our *Church Chronicle* were published by Dr. Joseph Beck, in 1883, under the title *Geschichtsbuecher der Wiedertaeufer*. Our history is written with blood and tears; it is largely a story of persecution and suffering. We have record of over two thousand persons of our faith who suffered martyrdom by fire, water, and the sword. Our Church has been driven from country to country, and rather than to compromise their principles, have fled to various countries until at last they emigrated from Russia to this country in 1874.

We would further say that we love our country and are profoundly thankful to God and to our authorities for the liberty of conscience which we have hitherto enjoyed. We are loyal to our God-ordained government and desire to serve our country in ways and duties which do not interfere with our religious convictions. We humbly ask you, our dear Mr. President, not to lay upon us any duties which would violate our Christian convictions, and we hope, you believe with us, that we ought to be faithful to the teaching of God's Word and the dictates of our conscience, and should suffer what He may permit, rather than to do that which we clearly recognized to be contrary to His Word.

Dear Mr. President, we humbly ask that we may be permitted the liberty to live according to the dictates of our conscience as heretofore. With the vow of baptism we have promised God and the Church on bended knees to consecrate, give and devote ourselves, soul and body and all, to the Lord in heaven, to serve Him in the way which, according to His Word we conceive to be acceptable to Him. We humbly petition our Honored Chief Executive that we may not be asked to become disobedient to Christ and His Church, being fully resolved, through the help and grace of God, to suffer affliction, or exile, as did our ancestors in the times of religious intolerance, rather than violate our conscience or convictions and be found guilty before our God.

For proof that our attitude on the points in question is one of conviction, and not of arbitrariness, we would respectfully refer you to our *Confession* mentioned above, as well as to our life and history. We desire to serve our country and be respectful and submissive in every way not interfering with serving our God consistently. We are sincerely thankful for having been granted shelter and protection by our government and for having enjoyed full religious freedom up to the present time, and are quite willing to do something for the good of our country, provided that it is not against our conscientious convictions.

Very respectfully yours,
Hutterian Brethren Church

David Hofer.
Elias Walter.
Joseph Kleinsasser.

APPENDIX F

ARTICLES OF INCORPORATION


Approved As To Form and Filed
May 10, 1960
Victor A. Meyers
Secretary of State


ARTICLES OF INCORPORATION OF
HUTTERIAN BRETHREN OF SPOKANE, INC.

KNOW ALL MEN BY THESE PRESENTS, That, we the undersigned, each being of full age and citizens of the United States have associated ourselves together for the purpose of forming a corporation for a church of Spokane, Spokane County, Washington, under chapter R.C.W. 24.08 of the Laws of the State of Washington governing religious corporations, and to that end, and for that purpose, we do hereby sign and acknowledge the following Articles of Incorporation in triplicate and do state as follows:

ARTICLE I
NAME AND PLACE OF BUSINESS

Section 1. The name by which this corporation shall be known is Hutterian Brethren of Spokane, Inc.

Section 2. The place of business is located in the City of Spokane, c/o 212 Symons Building, Spokane County, Washington

ARTICLE II
MEMBERSHIP

Section 1. Members shall be chosen and elected to membership in the said Church upon the majority vote of the active members present and voting, at any annual, general or special meeting of the said body.

Section 2. Active members shall be the voting members of the body and shall be all male persons who have been Baptized and Confirmed in the Hutterian Brethren Faith and have signed the Membership Compensation Roll of the body.

Section 3. Inactive members shall be all other persons in said body, including infants from moment of birth, whose names appear on the Church Book.

Section 4. Any member of said body may be expelled or dismissed from said body at any annual or general meeting of said body, upon (1) two-thirds vote of the voting members thereof, (2) upon request of the member; or by leaving or abonding [sic] the body, (3) refusing to obey the rules and regulations, By-Laws and officers of said body, or (4) failing to give and devote all his time, labor, services, earnings and energies to the said body and purposes thereof, (5) failing to do and perform the work, labor, acts and things reguired [sic] of him or her by said body; or (6) failing to attend and engage in the regular meetings, worship and services of the members of the said body, and such dismissal shall be final and conclusive.

## ARTICLE III
## OBJECTS AND PURPOSES

Section 1. The objects for which this corporation are formed shall be:

(a) Religious, benevolent, provident, educational and to promote, engage in and carry on the Christian religion and religious teachings and connected therewith, and as a part thereof, and of the religion and religious teachings and belief of the members of the said religious body, to engage in, carry on and conduct farming, agriculture, milling, manufacturing of flour and other articles from agricultural products, and mechanics and mechanical arts necessary thereto, and to buy, sell and deal in said agricultural products and products made and manufactured therefrom, and other articles, material, machinery, implements and things belonging to, or necessary to engage in, carry on, and conduct said farming, agriculture, milling, manufacturing, mechanic and mechanical arts necessary thereto, and as part of and connected with the religion and religious teachings of said body and members thereof.

(b) That all the property, real and personal, of said body howsoever it may have been obtained, shall forever be owned, used, occupied and possessed by said body for the common use, interest and benefit of each and all the members thereof, for the purposes of said body during the time, and so long as they remain members thereof.

(c) That all the property, both real and personal, that each and every member of the said body have, or may have, own, possess or be entitled to at the time that they join such body, or become members thereof, and all the property, both real and personal, that each and every member of said body may have, obtain, inherit, possess, or be entitled to, after they become members of said body to be owned, used, occupied and possessed by said body for the Common use, interest and benefit, of each and all of the members thereof as aforesaid.

(d) That each and every member of said body shall give and devote all of his or her time, labor, services, earnings and energies to said body, and the purposes for which it is formed, freely, voluntarily and without compensation or reward of any kind whatever other than hereinafter expressed.

## ARTICLE IV
### TRUSTEES AND OFFICERS

Section 1. This corporation shall be managed by a board of not less than three nor more than seven members, as specified in the By-Laws of this corporation, with the principal officer to be known as Chairman, Vice-Chairman and Secretary-Treasurer and the balance, if any, to be Trustees.

Section 2. The secular business of the corporation shall be managed by the Board of Trustees, each of whom shall be not less than 21 years of age and shall be elected by the voting members of the body at the annual meeting to hold office for a period of one year, or until their successors are elected and qualify.

Section 3. VACANCY. Any vacancy therein shall be filled by vote of two-thirds of the members of the said body in a duly constituted meeting.

Section 4. OFFICERS. The Board of Trustees shall elect from their membership to hold office for a term of one year, or until their successor shall be elected, a chairman, a vice-chairman and a secretary-treasurer and the duties of each officer shall be governed by the By-Laws of this corporation.

The names and addresses of the incorporators of this corporation abd [sic] the first Board of Trustees thereof are as follows:

Paul S. Gross, Chairman, Lind, Washington;

Jacob Wollman, Vice-Chairman, Lind, Washington;

Eli Wollman, Secretary-treasurer, Lind, Washington.

and that their term of office shall be for a term of one year from date of incorporation, or until their successors have been elected and qualify.

## ARTICLE V

Section 1. The meetings of the Board of Trustees shall be as specified in the By-Laws and the annual meeting of the membership shall be on the first Monday in January at 10 o'clock a.m. in the office of the corporation.

## ARTICLE VI
### BY-LAWS, RULES AND REGULATIONS

Section 1. This corporation is empowered to make by-laws, rules and regulations.

## ARTICLE VII
### AMENDMENTS

Section 1. These articles of incorporation may be amended by a majority vote of those voting members present at a meeting called for the purpose after at least ten days written notice thereof to all members as shown on the membership roll of said church.

Section 2. IN WITNESS WHEREOF, we, the undersigned, have hereunto set our hands and seals this 30th day of January, 1960.


_____

Paul S. Gross - Chairman


_____

Jacob Wollman - Vice Chairman


_____

Eli Wollman - Secretary-Treasurer


STATE OF WASHINGTON

County of Adams

I, the undersigned, as a Notary Public in and for the State of Washington, do hereby certify that on this 30th day of January, 1960, personally appeared before me Paul S. Gross, Jacob Wollman, and Eli Wollman to me known to be the persons whose names are subscribed in the foregoing instrument and duly acknowledged to me that they executed the same as their free and voluntary act indeed for the uses and purposes therein mentioned.

GIVEN under my hand and official seal the day and year in this certificate first above written.


                              _____Leonard F. Jansen_____
                              Notary Public in and for
                              the State of Washington,
                              residing at Ritzville.

## APPENDIX G

### HUTTERITE SERMON

The sermon plays a vital role in the ritual life of the Hutterites. Sermons are invoked at every spiritual service, every day, including Sunday. Some are short, others quite long. There are sermons which are read at special times during the liturgical year, such as Advent, Christmas, Easter and Pentecost. Others are designated for occasions marking significant rites of passage, such as baptism, marriage, and death. Many sermons have no specific significance as to the occasions at which they are read. These are selected at the discretion of the minister. All Hutterian sermons, however, generate a deep sense of spirituality characteristic of the Hutterite's devotional life. Sermons are conservative interpretations of scriptural texts; they are, in essence, exegetic works. They are read, not in an emotional manner, but rather with a hortatory sense of admonishment. They serve to impart the "true" meaning of the Bible verses about which they were written.

When the Brethren gather for a religious service, the minister enters the meeting room, followed by the various elders and the men who hold colony offices. These men take their seats at the front of the room, facing the congregation, who follow in a prescribed manner: men first, women next, and then unbaptized boys and girls. All of the membership are seated according to sex and age.

When the minister reads the Bible text of the sermon, in a chanting manner, all present in the room stand. When he is finished reading, the membership sits and the interpretive sermon begins.

The spiritual nature of Hutterianism is manifest in its sermons. The following sermon, one of the nearly 300 in Paul Gross's collection, stands out as one of the few Hutterite sermons ever to be translated. It is perhaps best appreciated by being read in its entirety.

### SERMON ON I THESSALONIANS 5:1-11

*(1) "But of the times and the seasons, brethren, ye have no need that I write unto you."*

Paul, the enlightened apostle, tells us in the preceding fourth chapter, how it will be with the dead and their Resurrection. Namely, that they will be quickened with the trumpets of God and go to meet the Lord in the clouds and be judged. Then the believing Thessalonians no doubt wanted to know at what time and hour this would happen, whereupon he [the Apostle] told them these words we have just heard in text: "But of the times and the seasons, Brethren, ye have no need that I write unto you." But here the Apostle conforms to the model and example of Jesus Christ, who said unto his disciples: "Heaven and earth shall pass away, but my words shall not pass away. But of that day and hour knoweth no man, no, not the angels of heaven, but my Father only" (Matt. 24:35). Now, somebody might think or say: Why is it useless or unnecessary to know the day of the coming of Christ, and why has God preserved that secret in his power alone? Unto him be the answer: So that men may never live securely or without cares, but rather, every hour and moment keep themselves judged and prepared, with piety and righteousness and with a blameless life. As Christ also teaches, "Let your loins be girded about, and your lights burning; and ye yourselves like unto men that wait for their lord, when he will return from the wedding; that when he cometh and knocketh, they may open unto him immediately. Blessed are those servants, whom the lord when he cometh shall find watching: verily I say unto you, that he shall gird himself, and make them to sit down to meat, and will come forth and serve them. And if he shall come in the second watch, or come in the third watch, and find them so, blessed are those servants. And this know, that if the goodman of the house had known what hour the thief would come, he would have watched, and not have suffered his house to be broken through. Be ye therefore ready also; for the Son of man cometh at an hour when ye think not" (Luke 12:35-40). For without doubt, if men knew their last hour, and knew when they would die, or how long they still have to live, then most of them would think: "I still have time for repentance! I will first, because I am still young, serve my flesh and wait with my repentance. Afterwards, when I am no longer able and am old, I will serve God and prepare myself to repentance." But this will not count before God and he will have no pleasure in such repentance. For that man who spends his youth in sin and seeks to please the devil, and only later in his old age wants to repent and serve God, does the same as if he offered the wheat to Satan and the chaff to the Lord. Or as if a cup-bearer would drink off the best wine and give his master the leftovers and the dregs. That would be an unfaithful servant, and would receive an evil reward. Therefore it is good that God has hidden from men his end and the hour of His judgment, for that gives him a reason never to be safe and secure, but to be prepared every hour and moment. For, to speak in a parable, if in a city the arrival of an emperor or king is awaited, but the exact day and hour of his arrival is not known, nevertheless everyone is busily occupied with preparations; everybody is busy repairing the roads and streets as if his approach were due any minute. Thus and a thousand times more should we prepare and ready ourselves for the arrival of our Lord Jesus Christ, that we may be worthy to stand before his face, even though we are uncertain of the day and hour of his coming. Therefore he says: "Behold, I come as a thief. Blessed is he that watcheth, and keepeth his garments, lest he walk naked, and they see his shame" (Rev. 16:15).

*(2) "For yourselves know perfectly that the day of the Lord so cometh as a thief in the night."*

Here Paul is saying: You believers have been sufficiently convinced from the Holy Scriptures, and assured in your hearts in what form Christ will come and appear in his judgment. Therefore you need nothing but to watch and stand prepared; he may come afterwards whenever he wishes – in the evening, at midnight, at cockcrow or in the morning, that you might be found prepared. For all who are unprepared will fare as the unworthy guest (Matt. 22:11), or the unprofitable servant (Matt. 25:30), or the foolish virgins (Matt. 25:12). The Lord says: "And it shall come to pass at that time, that I will search Jerusalem with candles, and punish the men that are settled on their lees: that say in their heart, The Lord will not do good, neither will he do evil . . . The great day of the Lord is near . . . and hasteth greatly, even the voice of the day of the Lord: the mighty man shall cry there bitterly. That day is a day of wrath, a day of trouble and distress, a day of wasteness and desolation, a day of the trumpet and alarm against the fenced cities, and against the high towers. And I will bring distress upon men, that they shall walk like blind men, because they have sinned against the Lord" (Zeph. 1:12, 14-17). Paul, the Apostle says: "When the Lord Jesus shall be revealed from heaven with his mighty angels, in flaming fire taking vengeance on them that know not God, and that obey not the gospel of our Lord Jesus Christ; who shall be punished with everlasting destruction from the presence of the Lord, and from the glory of his power; when he shall come to be glorified in his saints, and to be admired in all of them that believe (because our testimony among you was believed) in that day" (II Thess. 1:7-10). In Revelation the Spirit of God says: "Behold, he cometh with clouds; and every eye shall see him and they also which pierced him: and all kindreds of the earth shall wail because of him" (Rev. 1:7). Then everyone will fare well if he is faithful and well prepared. But eternal woe unto all the lazy, the half-hearted, and the sleepy.

*(3a) "For when they say, peace and safety; then sudden destruction cometh upon them."*

Christ says: "Now learn a parable of the fig tree. When his branch is yet tender, and putteth forth leaves, ye know that the summer is nigh. So likewise ye, when ye see all these things, know that it is near, even at the doors" (Matt. 24:32). Now we know that the security of which Paul here speaks, and the terrible seduction and blindness of which Christ speaks is manifest in our day and is in full momentum. Therefore nothing is more urgent at present than to lift our eyes and prepare ourselves; to remove the defiled garment of sins and clothe ourselves with the white garment of piety and innocence, that when the king shall come to see the guests, we may not be found as the unworthy guest, to whom the king said: "Friend, how camest thou in hither not having a wedding garment? And he was speechless. Then said the king to the servants: Bind him hand and foot, and take him away, and cast him into outer darkness; there shall be weeping and gnashing of teeth" (Matt. 22:12,13). He who puts off his preparation and repentance and changing his ways until sudden destruction comes upon him has waited too long and will find no more place for repentance (Heb. 12:17), but a terrible expectation of judgment and fiery indignation, which shall devour the wicked (Heb. 10:27). John writes in the Revelation: "And I saw another mighty angel come down from heaven, clothed with a cloud: and a rainbow was upon his head, and his face was as it were the sun, and his feet as pillars of fire: and he had in his hand a little book open, and he set his right foot upon the sea, and his left foot on the earth, and cried with a loud voice, as when a lion roareth; and when he had cried, seven thunders uttered their voices. And when the seven thunders had uttered their voices, I was about to write: and I heard a voice from heaven saying unto me, Seal up those things which the seven thunders uttered, and write them not. And the angel which I saw stand upon the sea and upon the earth lifted up his hand to heaven, and sware by him that liveth for ever and ever, who created heaven, and the things that therein are, and the earth, and the things that therein are, and the sea, and the things which are therein, that there should be time no longer: But in the days of the voice of the seventh angel, when he shall begin to sound, the mystery of God should be finished, as he hath declared to his servants, the prophets" (Rev. 10:1-7). Therefore, dear Brethren, let us do something about it, while it is called today (Heb. 3:13), while it is still the accepted time, and the day of salvation and while God still offers us his grace and his outstretched hand (II Cor. 6:2). Let us believe what the prophets, the apostles, the holy angels, and Christ, the Son of God have said, and not what the secure and wicked prophets and the world-of-today say. They [the latter] believe and allege that the world is not in danger, for they are all Christians. Christ has died for them and has paid for their sins; he will be faithful, they say, and will abide by his promise, for he says himself: "For God sent not his Son into the world to condemn the world; but that the world through him might be saved" (John 3:16). But they want, with the publican in the temple, only to smite upon their breast, saying, "God be merciful to me a sinner" (Luke 18:13); or with the thief on the cross, "Lord, remember me when thou comest into thy kingdom" (Luke 23:42).

In contrast, Christ and his apostles, like his faithful servants today, believe and preach that no sinner, nor unclean person, nor a man defiled by vice will see the kingdom of God without true repentance. And that one must repent, put way all sin, vice and all carnal works; hate himself, deny himself, and bear the cross of Christ and follow him (Matt. 16:24). "And whosoever he be of you that forsaketh not all that he hath . . ." (Luke 14:33) and "he that taketh not his cross, and followeth after me, is not worthy of me" (Matt: 10:38).

Paul says likewise: "Know ye not that the unrighteous shall not inherit the kingdom of God? Be not deceived; neither fornicators, nor idolaters, nor adulterers, nor effeminate, nor abusers of themselves with mankind, nor thieves, nor covetous, nor drunkards, nor revilers, nor extortioners shall inherit the kingdom of God" (I Cor. 6:9-10). He who does not believe that, and comforts himself with anything else, will be like the servant of whom Christ says: "But and if that evil servant shall say in his heart: My lord delayeth his coming; and shall begin to smite his fellow-servants, and to eat and drink with the drunken, the lord of that servant shall come in a day when he looketh not for him, and in an hour that he is not aware of, and shall cut him asunder, and appoint him his portion with the hypocrites: there shall be weeping and gnashing of teeth" (Matt. 24:48).

*(3b) "As travail upon a woman with child; and they shall not escape."*

With these words the apostle wants to tell us that the punishment, destruction and judgement of the ungodly will by no means fail to appear but will certainly come, even as certainly as labor pains upon a woman with child. The apostle wants to teach us that we should never feel too certain or become careless, but be on the watch at every hour and be prepared. For a woman with child, even though she does not know the day and hour when labor pains will come, has no doubts but readies and prepares herself as much as possible and as much as she can. For, even if we do not know the day and the hour in which God will appear with his judgment, we should conduct our lives as if he were to appear at any moment.

For he who wants to escape the destruction which will fall upon the ungodly at the end of the world must prepare himself now and be ready. He must forsake sin and the worldly life and have nothing to do with them. But he who cannot leave sin and unrighteousness in this life, but wilfully continues to allow it, and lives in it without ceasing, he will be caught with the world in its destruction and will be overcome by it. "Therefore shall her plagues come in one day, death, and mourning, and famine; and she shall be utterly burned with fire, for strong is the Lord God who judgeth her" (Rev. 18:8). "If any man worship the beast and his image, and receive his mark in his forehead, or in his hand, the same shall drink of the wine of the wrath of God, which is poured out without mixture into the cup of his indignation; and he shall be tormented with fire and brimstone in the presence of the Lamb: and the smoke of their torment ascendeth up for ever and ever, and they have no rest day nor night, who worship the beast and his image, and whosoever receiveth the mark of his name" (Rev. 14:9-11). And in another passage in his secret Revelation John writes: "And I saw a great white throne, and him that sat upon it, from whose face the earth and heaven fled away; and there was found no place for them. And I saw the dead, small and great, stand before God; and the books were opened: and another book was opened, which is the book of life: and the dead were judged out of those things which were written in the books, according to their works. And the sea gave up the dead which were in it; and death and hell delivered up the dead which were in them: and they were judged every man according to their works. And death and hell were cast into the lake of fire. This is the second death. And whosoever was not found written in the book of life was cast into the lake of fire" (Rev. 20:11-15). From here the people will try to escape, but will be unable to. For all the earth will be filled with the glory of God and his strength. "In those days shall men seek death, and shall not find it; and shall desire to die, and death shall flee from them" (Rev. 9:6). Instead they will have to wait with fear and trembling and will faint. Therefore it is not in vain that the Lord says: "Watch ye therefore, and pray always, that ye may be accounted worthy to escape all these things that shall come to pass, and to stand before the Son of Man" (Luke 21:36).

*(4) "But ye, brethren, are not in darkness, that that day shall overtake you as a thief."*

By darkness we understand all unrighteousness, all deeds and works which men do not openly expose in the light of the day; but only in secret, where no man sees their activity. In summary: No matter how small and unimportant a thing or deed may seem, if it is not done according to the proper order, or right usage, if it is not done honestly and openly, but secretly with cunning, with falsehood, and with deception, it is a work of darkness. But Paul teaches here, and also in other parts of his epistles, that we should not be involved in the works of darkness: "Let us therefore cast off the works of darkness, and let us put on the armour of light. Let us walk honestly, as in the day; not in rioting and drunkenness, not in chambering and wantonness, not in strife and envying" (Rom. 13:12-13). "For ye were sometimes darkness, but now are ye light in the Lord: walk as children of light. (For the fruit of the Spirit is in all goodness and righteousness and truth;) proving what is acceptable unto the Lord. And have no fellowship with the unfruitful works of darkness, but rather reprove them. For it is a shame even to speak of those things which are done by them in secret. But all things that are reproved are made manifest by the light; for whatsoever doth make manifest is light" (Eph. 5:8-13). And he who abides in this and fulfills it will not be seized or overtaken as a thief by the day of the Lord; but that day will be a paymaster, a rewarder, and a compensator. We can also interpret the words of the apostle, "But ye are not in darkness" to mean that we should not be ignorant and unlearned in the divine light and godly knowledge, but instead should be well-versed in the Word and Law, and have the proper knowledge of what is hateful, pleasing, or agreeable to him. For as little as the servant of an earthly lord can fulfill his master's will or act according to what pleases him, much less can a Christian or servant of God live in a way pleasing to God or fulfill the will of Christ, if he does not know God's will and is not instructed in the law of Christ. Therefore we have reason to pray to God, that he may open the eyes of our hearts; that he may give us power according to the "riches of his glory" (Eph. 3:16), to be strengthened with might by his Spirit in the inner man; that Christ may dwell in our hearts by faith; "that ye, being rooted and grounded in love, may be able to comprehend with all saints what is the breadth, and length, and depth, and height; and to know the love of Christ, which passeth knowledge, that ye might be filled with all the fulness of God" (Eph. 3:18-19).

*(5) "Ye are all the children of light, and the children of the day. We are not of the night, nor of the darkness."*

By conversion from the sinful life, to piety, godliness, and righteousness, and through honest repentance and reconciliation with God; indeed through the death and through the pardon of Christ, people who have been reconciled with God are released from the snares of hell and of darkness. Children of the devil have become children of God, and children of darkness, children of light. For John says: "That was the true Light, which lighteth every man that cometh into the world. He was in the world, and the world was made by him, and the world knew him not. He came unto his own, and his own received him not. But as many as received him, to them gave he power to become the Sons of God, even to them that believe on his name: which were born, not of blood, nor of the will of the flesh, nor of the will of man, but of God" (John 1:9-13).

Christ says: "I am come a light into the world, that whosoever believeth on me shall not abide in darkness" (John 12:46). But let no one draw a false comfort or a false hope out of it, that he should think or speak in his heart: "Now since I believe in Christ and have been baptized in his name and walk in and out among the saints, I am saved, and am free from the power of death and darkness. I have no need to worry about how I live or serve God!" For the words of our text: "Ye are all the children of light and the children of the day," are spoken by Paul only to those who yield to God in the proper manner: who have renounced serving the devil, the world, their own evil lusts, and have been reconciled with God. The works of darkness such as "adultery, fornication, uncleanness, lasciviousness, idolatry, witchcraft, hatred, variance, emulations, wrath, strife, seditions, heresies, envyings, murders, drunkenness, revellings, and such like: of the which I tell you before, as I have also told you in time past" (Gal. 5:19-21), shall no longer be seen, noticed or felt in them. Rather they are concerned with chastity and love toward God and conciliation towards their fellowmen, with moderation and temperance in eating and drinking; in summary, in their whole life they shall shine and let themselves be seen as a light in the world (Matt. 5:14-16). But those that only want to confess with their mouth that they know God, but in works deny him with a body that is to decompose and that has no value before God, and with the mind and heart, which should be offered to God they cling to the world (Titus 1:16). In summary: He who does not take pains to live and walk as the teaching of Christ enables and demands, as the duty of a Christian and brother in Christ, does not take comfort in these works of the Apostle Paul. For they walk in darkness and do not know whither they walk, for the darkness has blinded their eyes (I John 2:11). Only with their mouths forsaking the world and the works of darkness, and in their works running "with them to the same excess of riot" (I Peter 4:4), and still pulling with them in the yoke of unrighteousness (II Cor. 6:14), but they can have no validity before God. Much less can such an appearance and such hypocrisy bring salvation to anyone. For "that servant, which knew his lord's will, and prepared not himself, neither did according to his will, shall be beaten with many stripes" (Luke 12:47).

*(6) "Therefore let us not sleep, as do others; but let us watch and be sober."*
The Apostle is saying: Since we as believers and God-fearing have by the grace of God been saved from the powers of the devil and from the snares of sin and

darkness, and because to us above all other nations God's will, his light and knowledge have been revealed and made manifest: it is no longer right that we should live and walk without knowledge of God and attentiveness to God like the others, to whom God's will is not revealed, but concealed. Instead, it is demanded of us that we, with watching and praying, with resistance to sin, and with mortifying and renouncing of sinful lusts and of the old man, shall not be defeated, but advance with all earnestness and zeal and pursue holiness to attain it.

Paul also teaches this in another passage: "Finally, my brethren, be strong in the Lord, and in the power of his might. Put on the whole armour of God, that ye may be able to stand against the wiles of the devil. For we wrestle not against flesh and blood, but against principalities, against powers, against the rules of the darkness of this world, against spiritual wickedness in high places. Wherefore take unto you the whole armour of God, that ye may be able to withstand in the evil day, and having done all, to stand. Stand therefore, having your loins girt about with truth; And having on the breastplate of righteousness; and your feet shod with the preparation of the gospel of peace; above all, taking the shield of faith, wherewith ye shall be able to quench all the fiery darts of the wicked. And take the helmet of salvation, and the sword of the Spirit, which is the word of God: praying always with all prayer and supplication in the Spirit, and watching thereunto with all perseverance and supplication for all saints" (Eph. 6:10-18). But he who has a stained heart, that is attracted and bewitched by fleshly lusts, by gluttony, drunkenness, lying and deception, envy, hate, with wrath, vengefulness, with false evil report and with slander, such a one is not watching but is sleeping (Gal. 5:19-21). The Word of God calls to such a person: "Awake thou that sleepest, and arise from the dead, and Christ shall give thee light" (Eph. 5:14). Another Scripture tells us: "I know thy works, that thou hast a name that thou livest, and art dead. Be watchful, and strengthen the things which remain, that are ready to die; for I have not found thy works perfect before God. Remember therefore how thou hast received and heard, and hold fast, and repent. If therefore thou shalt not watch, I will come on thee as a thief, and thou shalt not know what hour I will come upon thee" (Rev. 3:1-3).


*(7,8a) "For they that sleep sleep in the night; and they that be drunken are drunken in the night. But let us, who are of the day, be sober."*

By those that sleep, we understand all wicked and sinful people who continue to live without a conscience and without sensitivity, in blindness and ignorance, without the knowledge of God. Of such people, Paul says: "Having their understanding darkened, being alienated from the life of God through the ignorance that is in them, because of the blindness of their heart: who being past feeling have given themselves over unto lasciviousness, to work all uncleanness with greediness" (Eph. 4:18-19).

By the drunken ones we understand all those that are led astray by false doctrine and are ensnared and entrapped by close-mindedness and unbelief in their hearts. The night is the time of ignorance and lack of judgment in man before he is enlightened and understands God's will and pleasure. Therefore, Paul is saying in these words of our text: "For they that sleep sleep in the night; and they that be drunken, are drunken in the night," and indicating that those who live to find pleasure in sin and evil lusts and temptations and let the sin reign in them, who serve sin and carry out all sorts of vice and abomination without a thought and without disturbing their conscience (Rom. 6:12), have been misled and are being misled. "And even as they did not like to retain God in their knowledge, God gave them over to a reprobate mind, to do those things which are not convenient; being filled with all unrighteousness" (Rom. 1:28-29). But we, the Apostle is saying, who are enlightened by the Word of God and have been awakened from the slumber of sin, and to whom God has revealed his will and pleasure, should no longer walk without the knowledge of God or attention to God, following only our blind nature. No, rather, it is with a proper attention to the will and command of God, and with a proper recognition and knowledge of what is pleasing and acceptable to God, that we should lead our lives and walk before God. It is bad enough that we should remember how, before our conversion, we lived contrary to God and his will (I Pet. 4:3). But we are commanded: "Let not sin therefore reign in your mortal body, that ye should obey it in the lusts thereof. Neither yield ye your members as instruments of unrighteousness unto sin: but yield yourselves unto God, as those that are alive from the dead, and your members as instruments of righteousness unto God" (Rom. 6:12-12). For "he that saith, I know him, and keepeth not his commandments, is a liar, and the truth is not in him. But whoso keepeth his word, in him verily is the love of God perfected: hereby know we that we are in him. He that saith he abideth in him ought himself also so to walk, even as he walked" (I John 2:4-6).

Paul says in another passage: "Walk in the Spirit, and ye shall not fulfil the lust of the flesh. For the flesh lusteth against the Spirit, and the Spirit against the flesh: and these are contrary the one to the other: so that ye cannot do the things that ye would" (Gal. 5:16-17). In this passage Paul is teaching us that we would beware of idleness, gluttony, and drunkenness, but live in truth and sobriety. For through drunkenness, man becomes careless, impudent, and a forgetter of God, so that he forgets all modesty, propriety and decency, fearing neither God nor man. Examples can be seen in King Belshazzar and Holofernes, and today in many thousands of people (Dan. 5, and Jth. 13). Therefore, all who desire salvation, have reason to heed the teachings of the Apostle who says: "And be not drunk with wine, wherein is excess; but be filled with the Spirit" (Eph. 5:18). Christ teaches us also: "And take heed to yourselves, lest at any time your hearts be charged with surfeiting, and drunkenness, and cares of this life, and so that day come upon you unawares. For as a snare shall it come on all them that dwell on the face of the whole earth" (Luke 21: 34-35). And as a Christian is responsible and obligated to guard against overindulgence in eating and drinking, so is he obligated to guard himself against idleness and indolence, both in temporal and spiritual works. For Solomon says in his Proverbs: "I went by the field of the slothful, and by the vineyard of the man void of understanding; and, lo, it was all grown over with thorns, and nettles had covered the face thereof, and the stone wall thereof was broken down. Then I saw, and considered it well: I looked upon it, and received instruction. Yet a little sleep, a little slumber, a little folding of the hands to sleep: so shall thy poverty come as one that traveleth; and thy want as an armed man" (Prov. 24:30-34). The same thing happened to the five foolish and sleepy virgins (Matt. 25:1-13) and the wicked slothful servant (Matt. 25:26-30). "Go to the ant, thou sluggard; consider her ways, and be wise. Which having no guide, overseer, or ruler, provideth her meat in the summer, and gathereth her food in the harvest. How long wilt thou sleep, O sluggard? When wilt thou arise out of thy sleep?" (Prov. 6:6-9).

*(8b) "Putting on the breastplate of faith and love."*

That is, we should see to it that we are true lovers of God, and that we with faith and confidence in God, should keep ourselves prepared. Just like a soldier who arms himself for battle with the weapons of his knighthood, putting on his leg armor, his body armor, and his breast armor, which is his coat-of-mail – just so we, the knights and warriors of the Kingdom of God, should put on the armor of God. For like the breastplate or armor that protects against all dangerous wounds, faith and love protect us from the attacks of the enemy and give us an undaunted heart.

Therefore John says: "And this is the victory that overcometh the world, even our faith" (I John 5:4). But how is it our victory? This is how: If the world seeks to take a person's life, and tries to destroy him on account of his faith, then he has faith that he will receive a much better and everlasting life in its stead and this secures his victory. If the riches of this world tempt him to turn away from God, he believes that he can expect still greater riches from God. If he is tempted by the pleasures of this world, he knows and believes that he will experience greater happiness if he remains true to God. If the favor of this world is portrayed to him, he believes that the favor and grace of God is a thousand times better. So in this way he attains victory through his faith. But when one does not put on the breastplate of faith and love, his heart is soon wounded and pierced, so that he thinks, "What shall I do? I am not living right! I am not God-fearing; I have no faith, why should I longer tarry!" But he who is equipped with the breastplate or armor of faith and love, cannot be won by the devil into his snare and lusts.

*(8c) "And for an helmet, the hope of salvation."*

That is, with a firm confidence and an assured hope, and a confident trust in the kingdom of God and the eternal joys. He who has this positive assurance of his salvation is well equipped. He who cannot have this living hope is in dire need. The armed men of this world wear the helmet, that is a hard metal hat or head armor, by which the head is protected. If the head is protected, there is less danger to the body. So it is with the living hope of salvation. He who has it can boldly go forward thinking: "I cannot fail! I can win honor and blessing in eternity." He has a heart that remains steadfast. He can fight like a man and a knight under the flag of the great field marshal, Jesus Christ, in his armor of God. And this hope does not become shame (Rom. 5:5).

*(9) "For God hath not appointed us to wrath, but to obtain salvation by our Lord Jesus Christ."*

Paul is saying that God the Almighty has not ordained or chosen us for disgrace and punishment, but that we should obtain the fullness of our inheritance and the everlasting life through our only Ruler, God's Anointed, the Savior of mankind. We are now concerned about our salvation. Therefore we fight, struggle, endure and suffer. He who remains steadfast and true until death shall receive the crown of life (James 1:12). He will receive the palm branches on Mount Zion which shall be given to him by the Son of God, Jesus Christ, our Redeemer (I Peter 5:4).

*(10a) "Who died for us."*

Who suffered for us the most painful death; and was crucified for our sins, and has made a sacrifice for us that will last forever (Heb. 10:10-14; Eph. 5:2). He did not do that for his own sake. No, he did it for our sake alone, out of true love (I Pet. 2:24). For God "hath laid on him the iniquity of us all . . . and with his stripes we are healed" (Isaiah 53:6,5).

*(10b) "That whether we wake or sleep, or should live together with him."*

This is the equivalent of what the Apostle states in another reference: "Whether present or absent" (II Cor. 5:9), in this life, or taken away to our everlasting rest, we are partakers with Christ in eternal life and joy, according to the covenant and faith in Christ. "For none of us liveth to himself, and no man dieth to himself. For whether we live, we live unto the Lord; and whether we die, we die unto the Lord; whether we live therefore, or die, we are the Lord's. For to this end Christ both died, and rose, and revived, that he might be Lord of the dead and living" (Rom. 14:7-9).

*(11a) "Wherefore comfort yourselves together."*

In Hebrews, chapter 10 (verse 25), the Apostle says: "Exhort one another" every day. Here each one admonishes and thinks about the other one. How shall we admonish one another? As Moses, the servant of the Lord, admonished the children of Israel that they should keep His commandments and the law (Lev. chapters: 6, 7, 12, 13, 14; Deut. chapters: 6, 7, 27, 31); as the mother of the seven sons admonished them (II Macc. 7:1-41); as Mattathias admonished his sons, saying: "And now, my children, be ye zealous for the law, and give your lives for the covenant of your fathers. And call to remembrance the deeds of our fathers which they did in their generations; and receive great glory, and an everlasting name" (I Macc. 2:50-51). And in this manner the saints are to admonish one another that they might remain firm and strong in their faith; that we may be awake to the greatness which God offers (Eph. 1:19; Col. 2:19).

*(11b) "And edify one another, even as also ye do."*

Support each other in the faith; seek to be a good example and model to one another, that you may be a comfort and source of strength to each other. Be good builders in the house of the Lord; for a dilapidated house or building can often stand much longer if it is built upon and kept in repair. Even though it appears that it will soon collapse it could still stand for ten years or more if one is willing to make the effort to repair it. In the same way, if we build and support each other, many a member will be preserved, even though at times the outlook seems bad. Therefore, the Apostle means to say: Apply your best effort to support and edify one another, and lead one another to the Lord. Although we should build, it would be a sad state of affairs if one tore down and spoiled what others have built (Gal. 2:18). Therefore one should take great heed, as dear as one's salvation is, not to provoke anyone or be a hindrance to his salvation. For Christ pronounces woe and a curse on him who tears down, destroys his fellow man and causes him to stumble (Matt. 18:6,7). Therefore let us follow the Apostle Paul's instruction: "Let us draw near with a true heart in full assurance of faith, having our hearts sprinkled from an evil conscience, and our bodies washed with pure water. Let us hold fast the profession of our faith without wavering; for he is faithful that promised; and let us consider one another to provoke unto love and to good works: not forsaking the assembling of ourselves together, as the manner of some is; but exhorting one another: and so much the more, as ye see the day approaching" (Heb. 10:22-25). The Spirit says in the book of Revelation: "And, behold, I come quickly; and my reward is with me, to give every man according as his work shall be" (Rev. 22:12). And again we read: "The Son of man shall send forth his angels, and they shall gather out of his kingdom all things that offend, and them which do iniquity; and shall cast them into a furnace of fire; there shall be wailing and gnashing of teeth. Then shall the righteous shine forth as the son in the kingdom of their Father. Who hath ears to hear, let him hear" (Matt. 13:41-43). May the gracious Father in heaven, through his great mercy, make us all worthy and fit "to stand before the Son of Man" (Luke 21:36) on that great day, and to say with great joy: "This is our God, in whom we have hoped." Amen

Reprint:        Paul S. Gross and Elizabeth Bender, "A Hutterite Sermon of the Seventeenth Century," *Mennonite Quarterly Review*, XLIV (January, 1970), 59-71.

# BIBLIOGRAPHY

## PRIMARY SOURCES

**Manuscript Collections**

1.     Friedmann, Robert, MSS. Archives of the Mennonite Church, Goshen, IN. Hist. Mss. 1-404, General Correspondence: Box 8, Folder 16: Paul Gross, 1955-1963; Box 8, Folder 17: Paul Gross, 1964-1970.

2.     Gross, Leonard, MSS. Archives of the Mennonite Church, Goshen, IN. Executive Secretary Correspondence: Box 6, Folder 43: Paul Gross, 1971-

**Personal Correspondence**

1.     Hostetler, John, 4 letters, Feb.-Apr., 1992, to the author.

2.     Gross, Leonard, 3 letters, Feb.-Apr., 1992, to the author.

3.     Peter, Karl, 2 letters, March & May, 1992, to the author.

4.     Roth, John, 3 letters, Nov. 1991-May, 1992, to the author.

**Oral Interviews**

1.     Gross, Leonard, personal interviews, March 14-19, 1992, with the author.

2.     Gross, Paul S., personal interviews, November, 1991 - May, 1992, with the author.

3.     Gross, Sarah Anne, personal interviews, December, 1991 - May, 1992, with the author.

4.     Gross, William, personal interviews, October, 1991 - May, 1992, with the author.

5.     Jansen, Leonard, personal interview, April 8, 1992, with the author.

6.     Sloan, Stan, personal interview, March 7, 1992, with the author.

**Newspapers**

1.     Adams, Carlyle, "Our Religions: Hutterites," in *Spokane Daily Chronicle*, 30 November 1968.

2.  Barnes, Hazel, "Hutterite Colony Life Studied," in *Spokane Daily Chronicle*, 19 March 1970.

3.  Barnes, Hazel, "Hutterites follow pattern of First Christians," in *Spokane Daily Chronicle*, 28 June 1961.

4.  Barnes, Hazel, "Space Age Casts Shadow On Ancient Religious Sect," in *Spokane Daily Chronicle*, 27 June 1961.

5.  Barnes, Hazel, "Hutterites Run Modern Farm," in *Spokane Daily Chronicle*, 16 November 1977.

6.  Behrens, Tim, "Stewards of The Land," in *Spokesman-Review*, 16 September 1984.

7.  Erickson, Ruth, "Tells of Visit to Hutterian Brethren at Farm Near Reardan," *Davenport Times*, 22 December 1960.

8.  Glynn, James, "Hutterite Colony is Target of Property Law Proposal," in *Spokesman-Review*, 27 May 1962.

9.  "Hutterites Buy Land at Odessa," in *Spokesman-Review*, 18 March 1975.

10. "Hutterites Buy More Farm Land," in *Spokesman-Review*, 15 November, 1968.

11. "Hutterites Buy Tract for Colony," in *Spokane Daily Chronicle*, 18 March 1975.

12. "Hutterite Colonies Invite All Visitors," in *Spokesman-Review*, 9 May 1971.

13. "Hutterites Have Modern Dairy Farm Operation," in *Spokane Daily Chronicle*, 16 November 1977.

14. "Hutterites Loyal," in *Spokesman-Review*, 6 June 1962.

15. "Hutterites make Plans For Building," in *Spokesman-Review*, 1 July 1960.

16. "Hutterites Sell Irrigated Farm," in *Spokane Daily Chronicle*, 9 March 1963.

17. "Hutterite Views Incorrectly Interpreted, Group Holds," in *Spokesman-Review*, 17 June 1962.

18. "Limit-on-Land Proposal Eyed," in *Spokane Daily Chronicle*, 5 January 1963.

19. Nappi, Rebecca, "The Old School," in *Spokesman-Review*, 18 February 1990.

20.    Odean, Donna, "The Hutterites in Close-up," in *Spokesman-Review*, 14 November 1971.

21.    "Old Work, New World," in *Spokesman-Review*, 13 September 1981.

22.    "Palouse Profiles," in *Spokesman-Review*, 17 September 1984.

23.    "Probe into Sect's Land is Backed," in *Spokesman-Review*, 24 February 1963.

24.    Rice, Don, "Hutterite Group Settles near Lind, Seeks 'Only Peace'," in *Spokesman-Review*, 10 August 1956.

25.    Schmeltzer, Michael, "Christmas Tradition", in *Spokesman-Review*, 10 December 1983.

26.    Schmeltzer, Michael, "Colony Brings in Bumper Potato Crop," in *Spokesman-Review*, 14 October 1987.

27.    "Scholars Find Hutterites to be Most Prolific People," in *Spokesman-Review*, 7 December 1954.

28.    "Sect Plans Big Center," in *Spokane Daily Chronicle*, 1 July 1960.

29.    Tollefson, Ginger, "Hutterites Live In Peace," in *Easterner*, 25 November 1970.

30.    "Tour Includes Basin Colony," in *Spokane Daily Chronicle*, 1 August 1973.

**Public Documents**

1.    *Revised Code of Washington 1881*, ch. 24.08, sect. .025.

2.    Select Committee of the Assembly (Communal Property), *Report on Communal Property*, Edmonton, Alta: 1972.

3    State of Washington, Department of State, *Articles of Incorporation of Hutterian Brethren of Spokane, Inc.*, May 10, 1960, Ritzville, Adams County, Washington.

**Articles and Essays**

1.    Allard, W. A., "The Hutterites: Plain People of the West," *National Geographic*, 138, #1 (July, 1970), 98-125.

2.    Anderson, L. C., "The Hutterian Brethren With Emphasis on the South Dakota Schmiedeleut" (unpublished ms. 12th Annual Dakota History Conference, Madison, South Dakota, April 12, 1980).

3. Covert, N., "Hutterites Practice Different Type of Co-housing Development," *The Grange News*, (October, 1991), 7-8.

4. Easton, C., "A Touch of Innocence," *Westways*, 68, #12 (1976), 27-29.

5. Glick, I., "'Gelassenheit' – A Hutterite Tradition," *Ford-New Holland News*, 38, #2 (March, 1992), 4-9.

6. Gross, P., "A New Home in Washington State: Hutterite Colony finds New Acceptance, Opportunity in U.S.," *Mennonite Weekly Review*, (June 29, 1967), 9.

7. Gross, P., "A Pilgrim People: Expansion of Hutterite Colonies Prompted Numerous Migrations," *Mennonite Weekly Review*, (June 22, 1967), 13.

8. Gross, P., "The Geographical Expansian [sic] of the Hutterite Colonies" (unpublished address, National Historic Communal Societies Association, Yankton, South Dakota, October 6, 1989).

9. McAvory, S., "The Hutterites: An Unusually Modern Old-fashioned People," *Ruralite*, (August, 1973), 6-8.

10. McBride, S., "Old World Communal Life in a Modern Age," *Christian Science Monitor*, (October 21, 1977), 17-18.

11. "Metropolis Goes into Farming, While Century-old Commune Considers Getting Out," *Countryside and Small Stock Journal*, 71 (November-December, 1987), 46.

12. "Montana Communism Bible Style," *Northwest Rotogravure Magazine*, (January 6, 1957), 7.

13. Schmeltzer, M., "Hutterites: A People Apart," *Washington*, 3, #6 (March-April, 1987), 34-42, 65-67.

14. "The Promised Land," *Time*, (August 13, 1956), 24-26.

15. Thomas, V., "The Hutterites of Canada," *Gourmet*, (November, 1976), 32-36, 94-97, 102, 104, 106.

16. "Unlikely Conference Hosts," *Christianity Today*, 32 (September, 1988), 47.

**Books**

1. Anderson, Lawrence, *North American Hutterian Brethren*. By the author, n.d.

2. Barnett, D. C., and L. R. Knight, *The Hutterite People*. Saskatoon: Western Extension College Educational Publishers, 1977.

3. Bennett, John W., *Hutterian Brethren*. Stanford: Stanford University Press, 1967.

4. *The Chronicle of the Hutterian Brethren*, Vol. 1. Rifton, NY: Plough Publishing House, 1987.

5. Deets, L. E., *The Hutterites: A Study in Social Cohesion*. Philadelphia: Porcupine Press, 1975.

6. Eaton, J. W., and R. J. Weil, *Culture and Mental Disorders*. Glencoe, IL: The Free Press, 1955.

7. Eggers, U., *Community for Life*. Scottsdale, PA: Herald Press, 1988.

8. Flint, David, *The Hutterites: A Study in Prejudice*. Toronto: Oxford University Press, 1975.

9. Gross, P. S., *Pincher Creek Colony: Memories*. Pincher Creek, ALTA: By the author, n.d.

10. Gross, P. S., *The Hutterite Way*. Saskatoon: Freeman Publishing Company, Ltd., 1965.

11. Holzach, M., *The Forgotten People (Das vergessene Volk): A Year Among the Hutterites*. (Translated from the German by Stephan Lhotzky). Sioux Falls, SD: Ex Machina Publishing Company, 1993.

12. Hostetler, J., and G. Huntington, *The Hutterites in North America*. New York: Holt, Rinehart & Winston, 1967.

13. Ranke, H., *The Hutterites in Montana: An Economic Description*. Bozeman, MT: Montana State University, 1971.

14. Ridemann, P., *Confession of Faith*. London: Hodder & Stoughton; Rifton, NY: Plough Publishing House, 1950.

15. Riley, M., *South Dakota's Hutterite Colonies, 1874-1969*. Brookings, SD: South Dakota State University, 1970.

16. *Sermon Directory of the Hutterian Brethren*. 2nd edition, Reardan, WA: Spokane Hutterian Brethren, 1991.

17. Wiebe, F., trans., *The Martyrdom of Joseph and Michael Hofer, 1918*. Elkhart, IN: Associated Mennonite Biblical Seminaries, 1974, in Ziegelschmid, A. J. F., *Das Klein-Geschichtsbuch der Hutterischen Bruder*. Philadelphia: Carl Schurz Foundation, 1974. 482-486.

18. Wurtz, A., *The Memoirs of Reverend Andrew Wurtz: World War I – 1918: As Told to His Son Andrew A. Wurtz*. Warner, ALTA: Sunny Site Colony, n.d.

19.    Wurz, J. K., *The Hutterian Brethren of America*. Lethbridge, ALTA: By the author, 1968.

## SECONDARY SOURCES

**Periodicals**

1.    *Mennonite Quarterly Review*, since 1927: *passim.*

**Unpublished Monographs**

1.    *From Carinthia to Dakota: 1712-1874*. Goshen, IN: Mennonite Historical Library, call # M289.7H9/F931, n.d.

2.    Hege, A., *The Hutterites in the U.S.A.: A Religious Communitarian People*. Unpublished M.Litt. thesis, University of Strasbourg, 1974.

**Books**

1.    Dickens, A. G., *The Counter Reformation*. United Kingdom: Harcourt, Brace & World, Inc., 1969.

2.    Friedman, R., *Hutterite Studies*. Goshen, IN: Mennonite Historical Society, 1961.

3.    Gross, L., *The Golden Years of the Hutterites*. Scottsdale, PA: Herald Press, 1980.

4.    Gross, P., *Who Are the Hutterites*. Pincher Creek, ALTA: Mennonite Publishing House, n.d.

5.    Gross, P., *Why Community? The Ideal Communal Living*. Spokane: Spokane Hutterian Brethren, Inc., n.d.

6.    Gross, P., *Hutterian Brethren: Life and Religion*. Pincher Creek, ALTA: By the author, n.d.

7.    Gross, P., and Paula Thijssen, *Christian Community: The Outcome of Christian Belief*. Rifton, NY: The Plough, 1954.

8.    Hofer, J., *The History of the Hutterites*. Winnipeg: W. K. Printers' Aid, Ltd., 1982

9.     Horsch, J., *The Hutterian Brethren, 1528-1931: A story of Martyrdom and Loyalty.* Goshen, IN: Mennonite Historical Society, 1931.

10.    Hostetler, J., *Hutterite Life.* Scottsdale, PA: Herald Press, 1965.

11.    Hostetler, J., *Hutterite Society.* Baltimore: The Johns Hopkins University Press, 1974.

12.    Hostetler, J., *Communitarian Societies.* New York: Holt Rinehart & Winston, Inc., 1974.

13.    Hottman, H., *The Hutterites in South Dakota.* Mitchell, SD: Dakota Wesleyan University, 1990.

14.    Kephart, W., *Extraordinary Groups.* New York: St. Martin's Press, 1976.

15.    *The Mennonite Encyclopedia.* 5 Vols. Scottsdale, PA: Mennonite Publishing House, 1956, 1991.

16.    Peter, K., *The Dynamics of Hutterite Society.* Edmonton: The University of Alberta Press, 1987.

17.    Peters, V., *All Things Common: The Hutterian Way of Life.* Minneapolis: University of Minnesota Press, 1965.

18.    Ruth, J., *A Quiet and Peaceable Life.* Lancaster, PA: Good Books, 1979.

19.    Sitton, T., et al., *Oral History: A Guide for Teachers (and others).* Austin: University of Texas Press, 1983.

20.    Society of Brothers, *Children in Community.* Rifton, NY: The Plough Publishing House, 1963.

21.    Spradley, J., *The Ethnographic Interview.* New York: Holt Rinehart & Winston, 1979.

22.    Springer, N. P., and A. J. Klassen, comps., *Mennonite Bibliography: 1963-1961.* 2 Vols. Scottsdale, PA: Herald Press, 1977.

23.    Stephenson, P., *The Hutterian People: Ritual and Rebirth in the Evolution of Communal Life.* Lanham, MD: University Press of America, 1990.

# INDEX

Ukraine, 89, 95
  Hutterite migration to, 5, 15
United States, Hutterite migra-
  tion to, 5, 16, 17
*Vancouver Sun,* 98
Veterans Land Act (Canada), 55
Vishenka, Russia, 5, 30
*Wall Street Journal,* 98
Wages, absence of, 11,
Waldner, Johannes, 94-95
Waldner, Rev. Michael, 16
Wallachia, 4, 89
Walter, Darius, 16
Walter, Elias, 18, 22, 95
Warden Hutterian Brethren,
  83-84
Wartime Elections Act
  (Canada), 37, 57
Washington, 16, 55
  colonies, 85
  Hutterite migration to, 64-71
  land transactions, 68, 70, 77
  membership of first settle-
    ment, 68-69

Widemann, Jacob, 4
Wilson, Pres. Woodrow, 23, 34
  Hutterites' petition to, 22-23
Wipf, Jacob, 17, 24, 26-29
Wolf Creek Colony, 16, 20, 38
Wollman, Elias, 64, 65, 68, 70
  construction of Spokane
    Colony, 71-72
Wollman, Jacob, 53, 68, 70
Wollman, Sarah, 48, 59. *See
    also* Gross, Mrs. Paul S.
Women, members of workforce,
  10
World War I, 21-30, 37
World War II, 54, 87
Wurtz, Rev. Andrew, 24-26
Wurz, John, 60
Yankton, South Dakota, 30